RAPARAPA KULARR MARTUWARRA...

... All right, now we go 'side the river,
along that sundown way.

RAPARAPA
KULARR
MARTUWARRA

All right, now we go 'side the river,
along that sundown way.

Stories from the Fitzroy River Drovers

Acknowledgements

I wish to thank the Aboriginal Arts Board of the Australia Council for financial assistance to Raparapa Kularr Martuwarra.
The Battye Library, Photographic Section, State Library Service of Western Australia, generously gave time and permission for the use of extensive pictorial records. Thanks also to the Australian Institute of Aboriginal Studies, University of Western Australia Anthropology Department, to West Australian Newspapers and Bunuba Productions. The Aboriginal Development Commission (now ATSIC) supplied a superb array of photographs recently taken at Mt Barnett by Rod Taylor, to whom we also owe many thanks. Grateful acknowledgement is made to the communities of Mt Barnett (Kupungarri), and Gibb River stations for their co-operation in allowing the use of these photographs of current station work.
The language area map on p. 287 was devised by Bill McGregor, of Monash University. Landsat images of the Fitzroy River on pp.168-9 were provided by Remote Sensing Applications Centre, Dept Land Administration, W.A. Joyce Hudson provided helpful advice on correct spellings for the Aboriginal words in the text and maps. Nulungu College Broome assisted selection of photos with their facilities. Many others gave support and encouragement. Thanks to John Watson and other residents of Mt Anderson station; Peter Yu backed the project from the outset, Senator Georges provided office facilities, Sarah Yu, Ken Neilson and Steve Hawke advised on the manuscript, Kathy McDonald helped transcribe taped interviews, Merrilee Lands and Linda Wilmot read proofs. Thanks to many more, and to the staff of Magabala Books, who were a pleasure to work with.

P.M.

Published in Australia 1989
by Magabala Books,
P.O. Box 668, Broome, W.A. 6725
Reprinted with revisions 1993

Assisted by the National Aboriginal and Torres Strait Islander Bicentennial Program.

A project of the Kimberley Aboriginal Law and Culture Centre.

Production Editor, Design: Peter Bibby.
Contemporary photographers: Rod Taylor, Richard Andre, Maria Mann, Pamela Lofts, Paul Marshall and Ken Neilson. Line drawings by Pat Torres.
Maps on pp. 92-3,96,124-5,164-5 drawn by Paul Marshall.
Cover photographs: Richard Andre (B/W, superimposed), Pamela Lofts (Colour).
Typeset in Bookman.
Printed in Australia by Frank Daniels Pty Ltd, Perth.

National Library of Australia Cataloguing-in-Publication data:

Raparapa Kularr Martuwarra.

Includes index.
ISBN 0 7316 3328 8.

[1]. Aborigines, Australian – Western Australia – Kimberley – Biography. [2]. Aboriginal Australian stockmen – Western Australia – Kimberley – History. [3]. Aboriginal Australian stockmen – Western Australia – Kimberley – Biography. 4. Drovers – Western Australia – Kimberley – Biography. 5. Ranch life – Western Australia – Kimberley – History. I. Marshall, Paul, 1955– . II. Lawford, Eric, 1930– .

994.14

RAPARAPA KULARR MARTUWARRA

All right, now we go 'side the river,
along that sundown way.

Stories from the Fitzroy River Drovers

Eric Lawford, Jock Shandley, Jimmy Bird, Ivan Watson,
Peter Clancy, John Watson, Lochy Green, Harry Watson & Barney Barnes.

Edited by

Paul Marshall

Magabala Books

Kimberley, Wet Season.

Johnny Echo, Jimmy Olfin, Jimbo Johnson, Mt Barnett.   (Facing:) Desmond Bedford, Patrick Echo, Jeffrey Dutchie, Johnny Echo.

Foreword

The notion of this book was put to me in 1985 by John Watson. At the time he was chairman and executive officer of the Kimberley Land Council and I was his administrator. John is fluent in several of the Kimberley languages and well respected by his people, but in common with many of his generation he was not taught to read and write. Yet he was keen to see his elders gain recognition and respect for years of vital and demanding work. He wanted their account of things placed on the record. So I agreed to be their surrogate writer and the contributors were interviewed between November '86 and April '87. The transcripts from 14 hours of tapes were then edited to a narrative, with repetitions removed and passages dealing with the same theme drawn together.

English is a second language for these men of the North. Aboriginal English often uses pronunciation and grammar which the reader might find difficult to follow. We discussed this and their decision was to use standard English grammar in the written form. Every effort has been made to preserve the individual character of the storytellers. Each one of them had the final say on the content of his narrative.

The nine Aboriginal men who have contributed to this book come from different language groups (tribes) and different parts of the West Kimberley but they share a common background. They speak for whole generations that have endured injustices. The least we can do as a nation is to admit their account of events into our history.

Paul Marshall

Contents

Introduction

There are a lot of reasons why I've wanted to see a book like this one written. Firstly, I'm conscious of the false impression many people have of Aboriginal people today. A lot of tourists come up to the Kimberley, and they see Aboriginal people standing around the pub or shop, or sitting in a group under the trees. I know a lot of those people think, "Those Aborigines are a no-good people!" But the truth is, Aborigines aren't bad. Nobody has told those tourists the Aboriginal side of the story; they haven't heard how all those Aboriginal people came to be pensioned off. I'm interested in the welfare of those people. And I'm concerned that our children are missing out on the practical education that we received on the stations. Those stockwork and station skills just aren't being passed on, except in a few places. We're grateful for the photographs appearing in this book from Mt Barnett (Kupungarri) and Gibb River

Kurnangki Community, Fitzroy Crossing.

Jeffrey Dutchie in Mt Barnett Yard with greenhide twistrope.

communities, where Aboriginal people are now running their own stations. They show how well those traditions are being passed on to their young people, mustering and working with cattle in the yard.

Secondly, I think that it's important for the old people's stories to be recorded. I first realised the need for a book like this when I was chairman of the Kimberley Land Council; I realised that Aboriginal people just weren't getting any input into books recounting the history of the Kimberley. Those books that have been written are mostly about kartiyas (whitefellas) and what wonderful things they've done. Very little attention has been given to Aborigines in those books, except to paint them as the "hostile natives" who speared cattle.

There's been little mention in those books about the duties Aboriginal people were responsible for, as far as the meat and wool industries go. Aboriginal people were involved in most areas of station work. The majority of the stockmen in the Kimberley were Aborigines. They were very good stockmen too; and some of them proved themselves to be pretty reliable. The whitefellas admittedly

Stockmen on their mules at Moola Bulla Aboriginal station, 1916.

owned the stations but you'll find that, for many years, all the head stockmen were Aborigines. But none of those Aborigines have got any credit for that; the kartiya always seem to get the credit.

Someone read me a book once which had been written by a kartiya drover. I don't know how many years he drove cattle for, but he had written the book to suit himself. Although he always had

John Charles, Noonkanbah rodeo.

nine or ten Aboriginal drovers working with him, they didn't get much of a story, or much of a say, in his book. There were about 20 pages of Aboriginal story out of the 240 pages in the book. That made me very sad.

Next came the job of choosing the informants whose stories fill the following pages. I couldn't help but pick those people whom I'd come to know back in my childhood. I grew up on Mt Anderson station and I used to see the same drovers go past maybe five or six times a year. Those people deserve some credit for all they've done. I wanted to make sure that in this book they would get the chance to have their own say.

Raparapa might also give people a bit of background on why Aboriginal people are fighting for their land, why they're fighting to highlight their interests or their cause. Another reason for the book is the concern the old people feel about the way the names to places have been changed. The same thing has happened all along the river, from Bohemia Downs and Louisa Downs right through to Derby. The new owners of those pastoral leases saw fit to change the names of the different waterholes, or to change the pronunciation of them. Most of those waterholes and dry camps, the watching camps where cattle are held overnight, have got blackfella names, but those original names have just been cast aside. I'd like to see all those names recorded before they fade from memory. They are the proper names for those places, and we'd like to see them come back into use. I'm hopeful that the maps we've compiled for this book will be a step in that direction.

I think it's time history started to acknowledge the contribution Aboriginal people have made to the pastoral industry in northern Australia. In the early days Aboriginal people were forced into working on the stations, but they quickly became responsible workers upon whom the stations depended. The people who have given their stories for this book are all important people in their own right, and they were glad of the opportunity to pass their stories on to the younger generation. Old age is starting to catch up with them.

This book hasn't come from reading other books, it has come directly from the personal experiences of all the contributors. Jimmy

Bird is the oldest man in Derby and his story reaches right back to the early days. Chum Lee, who is talked about in a few of the stories, not only drove cattle along the Fitzroy, he also drove cattle down the Canning Stock Route with a camel pack. They might look old and ragged today but they are very experienced men.

I think their stories will be of interest to all, both city and country people. You can't judge a book by its cover, you have to open it up and see what's inside. In the same way you can't judge Aboriginal people by their appearance today, you have to open your mind to their experience. I hope the reader will do just that.

John Watson

Aubrey Lynch, Chairperson, Aboriginal Lands Trust, Sandra Brooking, Bantam Jutumarra, Junjuwa 1986.

Overleaf: Robert Brooking at the Noonkanbah rodeo, with Henry Skinner mounted on his right, John Bomalie on foot to his left.

xiii

RAPARAPA
KULARR
MARTUWARRA

All right, now we go 'side
the river, along that sundown way.

Northern rain.

Azaria Thomas.

CHAPTER 1

Crowbar saved my life

Eric Lawford

Walmajarri man (1930 -)

Yiji (Bush name)   Jangala (Skin name)

We'd wait till the cool of the late afternoon

I was born on the 15th of December, 1930 on Bohemia Downs
station. The Aboriginal name for that place is Kupatiya. My father
was old Bert Lawford, who at that time was both manager and a
part-owner of Bohemia Downs. He was a whitefella who had come
out from Mexico. I don't even know if Bert Lawford was his real
name, since a lot of the kartiya that came here in those days were
running from the law and went by assumed names.

I was 6 years old when I was taken away by the Fitzroy police. I was taken firstly to Fitzroy Crossing and then down to the Moore River settlement near Perth. Government policy in those days called for half-caste children to be taken away from their families and sent to government institutions. So my two brothers and I were sent down to Moore River, and my sisters were sent to Moola Bulla near Halls Creek.

When I was 14 years old I was allowed to leave Moore River and come back to the Kimberley, so I caught a boat to Broome and then got a ride on a truck back to Christmas Creek. They had given me a special pass which made me exempt from the provisions of the Act. It made me almost like a kartiya. I had drinking rights and I could travel where I wanted, but I had to live with the kartiya and act white. I wasn't permitted to live in the Aboriginal camps. I was allowed to visit my sisters at Moola Bulla, but I wasn't permitted to stay with them.

I started working at Christmas Creek station in '44 as a jackaroo, working under the older people. They taught me everything that I know. They taught me most of my stockwork; how to work cattle and all the jobs related to that. Old Barney Barnes and a few more of the old people are still alive, but a fair few have passed away now.

Moola Bulla. 1910-18 formal gathering at the meat gallows.

I was only 17 years old when I started running the camp at Christmas Creek. I was more or less the manager's yes-man; he'd tell me where to go and what to do, and I used to tell the others. All the good stockmen were supposed to be working under me, people like Tuluk Tighe, Chum Lee, and many of the old people here today. Well, they weren't so much under me as working with me. I used to listen more to what they told me than having to tell them anything. But the managers, as I've said, just used me as a yes-man. They told me to do this and to go there, and they expected me to tell all the stockmen. That's how the mustering was organised.

Life was pretty rough for us back then; it was hard in the stock camps. Hard all the time! We had to keep up with all the branding and get the bullocks mustered; and we always had to meet the manager's schedules. They used to reckon we were lazy if we couldn't brand about eight or nine thousand calves a year! We'd work from when the wet stopped right through till after Christmas, when the wet season came again. They used to let us go on holiday during the wet season. People used to go bush then, and live out in the bush until the stock camp started up. Then they'd come back and start all over again. That was usually around early March in the old days.

When I started work here, there were very few cattle and there weren't many improvements to the station. The billabong on the other side of the creek was the main waterhole on the station. There were hardly any bores. We had to build this station up again, more or less re-stock it. It was pretty hard work, but there were a lot of cattle that didn't die during the drought of 1945. We used to go out and bring cattle back from the frontier, as well as from Go Go, which was another station owned by the Emanuels. There were a lot of wild bullocks running out the back of Tonka. But then that area was all wild in those days!

The cattle were wild because a lot of bush blackfellas were living around there, people who'd come in from the desert. They'd spear the cattle and make them go even more wild. We could hardly control them! We started off rounding up maybe three or four hundred. Then we built that mob up until we were pretty well the best of the three Emanuel stations, as far as branding went. By the time I left, we were able to go out and brand 6,000 calves over the seven months from March till September. That was the average number that we'd brand; and we'd still have some clean-skins left over in September that we hadn't got around to branding.

Branding in the yards, Bohemia Downs, 1950s.

We used to be the first station to send cattle off to the meatworks each year. We'd start mustering before Go Go and Cherrabun, the other Emanuel stations. We built what they called a spell paddock at Christmas Creek, and we'd have over a thousand and maybe even fourteen hundred head mustered ready for when the meatworks opened in early April. Then we'd make up our numbers from the spell paddock and drove them to Broome or Derby.

The cattle were nursed more in those days. In some areas the cattle were quiet and in other areas they were wild, although they did go quiet once we'd handled them a bit and settled them down. You could ride a bronco horse through them then. The cattle were treated properly in those days too. The cattle were tailed and then they were settled down while we had our dinner. We'd wait till the cool of the late afternoon and then we'd cut the bullocks out, get the bronco horses, catch the calves and start branding them.

We used to improve the breed of our stock by spaying some of the cows. For example, if you had a herd consisting of red cattle and you wanted to keep to that breed, then you'd spay any animal with roan or white in it. We'd draft those cows out of the mob and take them up to the spaying crush. Tuluk Tighe, Chum Lee or King Goda used to do the spaying. Tuluk was our head spayer. They'd have all the tar ready and someone there to pass the needles and the spaying hook; and a solution of antiseptic so the spayer could wash his hands and the tools. They used a special hooked knife that's sharpened on the inside edge, and capped on the end to prevent accidental injury. That knife's edge was kept very sharp.

The spaying crush, Moola Bulla, 1910-18.

The first thing that Tuluk would do would be to mark the cow just behind the hip. When you look at a beast sideways you can see the hip-bone you know? Then he'd cut them just enough so that he could get his hand in, a cut about four inches long. Cut through the outer muscle and then break through the inner muscle. Then he'd be able to put his hand right in and feel along the hip-bone until he found the ovaries. He'd insert the spaying hook, cut the two ovaries out, and throw them away. Then he'd get someone else to sew the animal up, or if the others didn't know how to do it, he'd sew them up himself. Then someone would paint tar on the cut to prevent the flies blowing it. The spayed cows were usually kept separate for a week or so, until they recovered their strength.

Barney Yu, Nurrungurri, Gibb River.

Sometimes they'd muster the wild bush cows, old clean-skins. The stockmen would throw them, and then hold them down while someone spayed them on the ground. Since they didn't have cotton they'd have to cut some hair from the cow's tail to stitch the wound up. They called that bush spaying. They'd also cut a strip of skin from the cow's throat as a marker. It would heal open and leave the strip of skin hanging down. Otherwise they would have to earmark them. That way you'd know, when you mustered up next time, that they had already been spayed. It was surprising how many of those cows turned up. Stockmen reckon that bush spaying used to be fun.

They also used to knee string the wild bulls, which involved cutting some of the sinews on one front leg above the knee. It used to slow them down, since they only had three strong legs to run with. The bad leg threw them out of balance, so they didn't have an even speed and therefore they couldn't gallop. But you had to be wary when you were chasing a knee strung bull, because it throws its leg out to the side and could trip your horse.

It used to be good fun but it was also hard and dangerous work and people used to get hurt. I saw two stockmen get killed here, from falling off horses! And there are still a few people walking around here who've got broken legs and broken arms as a result of horse accidents. None of them received compensation. Nothing at all!

I remember seeing a young boy at a stock camp get his hand and arm chewed up by a donkey. Barney Barnes was breaking the donkey in and he had a young fella by the name of Mickey Thomas running around trying to grab it. But the donkey got its mouth around the boy's arm and started chewing. It only let go when Barney grabbed a stick and whacked it across the back of the neck, half killing it.

They took young Mickey back to the station and Vic Jones called the mail plane on the two-way. The mail plane picked him up and took him into Derby Hospital. Mickey Thomas is still alive today but his arm is badly scarred and isn't much use to him. I myself have been busted up three or four times from horse falls. I wasn't paid compensation. They might have paid my hospital bills but that's about it. A lot of blokes got no treatment at all.

Jeffrey Echo, Jimbo Johnson.

Johnny Malay, Alec Unengen (Jibudig), Jimbo Johnson.

I remember seeing this bloke by the name of Michaelangelo here in the stock camp with a broken arm. Nobody knew it was broken. He just thought it was swollen up. He was suffering from it until the next time the doctor came on his rounds, and informed him that he had a broken arm. It sort of just healed itself.

If the manager knew that someone had a broken arm, he'd usually just give him aspirin or something like that. The poor buggers! Only sometimes would they take an injured man into hospital. We didn't know much about the sort of treatment we should expect. The managers and owners were very tough in those days; they didn't care much about anybody's life. They were only interested in their bullocks!

I remember an accident I had myself. I was riding a colt out of the yard at Christmas Creek when the thing bucked me. As I fell off I was hit on the back of the head by a rock. But my foot was tangled up in the stirrup iron, and when that colt took off it started dragging me along beside it on the off-side, kicking out at me all the while in an effort to free itself. I didn't know what was going on since I was knocked out, but an old man called Crowbar saved my life. He was a real smart horseman and he was able to get his horse up to the near-side of the colt and jerk the stirrup leather out from under the saddle. I was pretty crook when I got up the next morning but I went straight back to the stock camp, since there was no chance of getting medical attention anyway. I jumped on another horse but I was thrown off again. I was pretty sick for a long time.

Soon as the hide came off a killer

Now I've been talking about myself, but a lot of these other people here could tell you a story or two. (At Wangkatjunga community, Christmas Creek - Ed.) There were people who got broken legs and were just left in the bush until somebody had time to come out and pick them up.

Kimberley early 20th C., young stockworker.

Not too far from Ngumpan here, down that range just over there, a young bloke had his leg broken right in half. The bone was sticking out, and his foot was at an odd angle to the leg. I wasn't in the stock camp at the time; I was off-siding with the windmill man at the station. Tuluk wasn't in the stock camp either, he was training horses at the time. Laidlaw was the manager at Christmas Creek then, so it would have been some time in the 'fifties.

Anyway, there was a kartiya cook out in the stock camp with them, but instead of the bastard taking the tractor out to pick that boy up, he drove the tractor into the station to tell the manager. When Stuart Hall and I weren't out working on the windmills we'd help out in the yard, and fortunately that's where we were on that day. Mrs Laidlaw was there and she sent me and Stuart out to pick the boy up in the Land Rover. I asked, "Why didn't that fucking tractor go out to where the boy was laying with his broken leg?" But that kartiya said he thought it might have been too rough! It was still pretty rough bringing him back to the station in the Land Rover, even on the mattress we took out with us. By the time Stuart and I got out there, Brumby Jack's mob had already made a splint for the boy out of bark and sticks, and carried him part of the way back to the station on a saddle horse. Fortunately they had aeroplanes up here by that time and they were able to radio the flying doctor to find out what should be done till the aeroplane came.

I mentioned that two stockmen were killed from horse accidents. Some of those men's children are walking around here today, and they didn't see any compensation for their fathers' deaths. They got no money. Nothing! I don't know if the station had any sort of insurance policy, but it seems like they didn't. If you fell down and broke your neck, you were gone; and none of the kartiya would worry about it! I don't think there was any welfare support in those days either.

We used to make our own ropes in the stock camps. As soon as we killed a beast, we'd cut the hide into strips and twist up the leather straight away. When I first came to Christmas Creek they had rope-makers working right throughout the wet season; old people like Lucky and that mob. They used to salt the hides and put them on tyres to dry. Then they'd cut them up and make either a plaited or twisted rope. Most of the ropes used to be the plaited type. All the old people used to make them; and they'd even take hair off the leather. But in the stock camps, as soon as the hide came off a killer, we'd twist it up and make head-ropes from it for use in the open bronco work. You know, for catching calves when the bronco time came. (Killer: cattle selected from the herd for station meat - Ed.)

Moola Bulla 1910-18, bush table for tanning hides.

Standard timber stockyard early 20th C.

After the stock camps finished up for the year we'd get onto the fencing work; putting up new fences and repairing the old fences. Then we'd do all the boundary riding over the wet. Blackfellas did all that work, not whiteman! Sometimes they might have had one whiteman working with all the old people. A lot of our old people used to work on those sort of jobs. The manager would have them cutting posts and rails with axes, carting them with the tractor and trailer, and putting them all in line where the yard was to be built.

About mid-November they'd put us into gangs down on the river and we'd be cutting posts and rails right up until Christmas. We'd cut 10 or 20 posts before smoko and 10 or 20 after smoko. All up we'd make perhaps 50 big posts in a day, as well as one or two hundred rails. And the next day we'd do the same thing. We'd be cutting them both for the yards and for the fences. Sometimes they would want a small horse paddock or yard built, and so we'd usually cut the posts and rails and build the thing, all in the same day.

This old man here, Tuluk Tighe, was the main horse-breaker for Christmas Creek. Sometimes he'd break-in as many as 50 horses in one year. He also used to train the manager's race horses. You know, train them for all the race meetings. We had a good breed of horses here for that sort of thing. The managers used to take the horses around to the race meetings and win money for themselves; but it was the blackfella that trained them. The blackfella would look after the horses, feed them, go everywhere with them. They'd stay with the horse until the race meeting had finished, but they didn't get any money for it!

Another job we had to do around the station was to keep up the maintenance on all the windmills. During the hot weather it was an early job nearly every day, going around to check all the windmills. If we found any that had broken down then we'd come back and get all the gear loaded into the vehicle. We did all the needed repairs on the spot. We'd have our dinner out there and come back to the station that night. Though sometimes we'd have to camp out there for two days so we could take all the column out, fix any broken rods, and get it all pumping again. There was a fair bit of work involved keeping those windmills in good order.

On Go Go station, prior to 1954.

Now in those days, to our experience, there was no such thing as money. We didn't see any money at all in the old days. All that the stockman got as pay was perhaps two shirts and two pair of trousers a year, while they were working. Boots, hat, canvas swag, and a couple of blankets were supplied too. That's about all. No money! The swags would usually last for two or three years. Anyone who owned a swag used to share it with those who didn't. We had a lot of kids in our stock camp, and if they had no boots or blankets then we used to give them whatever was spare.

When the wet season came and the people were allowed to go walkabout, they'd usually roll their swag up with the blankets and boots that the station had given them, and put it in the storeroom. Then they used to get their naga (loincloth) and go bush. When they came back the next year they'd go to the store and pick up their swags again for the mustering season. If they needed anything more then the station manager would give them another pair of boots, trousers, shirt or whatever.

The Government used to give the station owners or managers some sort of permit to work blackfellas such as myself and all the others here. That permit gave them the status of a "protector". It gave them the same authority as the policemen, who were also protectors. If there was any trouble with the blackfellas then the police used to be called in to sort it out. But, because he was the permit holder and as such a protector, the station manager could do pretty much as he liked.

That included the stealing of Aboriginal women. I remember when the Emanuels brought in the rule of not employing single managers, and requiring that all their managers who were single at the time find and marry a white woman. But in reality the Emanuels just brought in that rule to protect themselves. The rule only applied to the managers; there was no attempt to stop the kartiya stockmen and station hands from taking Aboriginal women.

The manager at Christmas Creek at the time was a bloke called Vic Jones. The Aborigines used to call him Milkin, or walking stick. Now, Vic Jones didn't like the new rule since he had taken an Aboriginal woman from the camp and already had one half-caste

Jock and Rita Shandley with family, dinner at Sandy Hill Billabong, the Noonkanbah rodeo.

kid by her. Because of the new rule he sent that kid over to Queensland. But then he ended up shooting himself, blew his brains out! His daughter came back and visited her mother only last year and took her over to Queensland for a holiday.

Women staff of Liveringa station, 1950s.

But the practice of kartiya men taking Aboriginal women didn't happen as much on Christmas Creek as it did on Go Go, or on the Vestey stations. You've got men from these stations even now living with Aboriginal women. There's one who's a project officer for DAA. (Dept. of Aboriginal Affairs - Ed.) He used to be a station hand in the old days. Those women that they are with were already married in the blackfella sense; they were promise-married. The way the old men see it, the feller who's the project officer now actually pinched that woman off her promised husband, a man from Brooking Springs station, or Kurang Ngatja in Aboriginal language. He's a young man who belongs to this country, one of the Christmas Creek mob.

16

Upper Liveringa station, early 20th C.

Albert Magic and John Watson when they were 19.

Kimberley outstation in the 1920s.

"Keep those cattle moving!"

They had station drovers on all the stations in those days, but sometimes the manager had trouble getting the numbers together to meet the shipment dates. So they'd send the head stockman with a mob, myself, Jock Shandley, or someone like that. Sometimes we'd take them all the way to Broome or Derby, or sometimes we'd meet up half way with another drover and hand them over to him. There would usually be five or six men in a droving plant, counting the cook. There would be three or four up front with the bullocks, the horse tailer behind them, and the cook would come along behind the horses with the donkeys.

After a while they put me on to droving more or less all the time. A few of us started contract droving, Tuluk, Wilfred, a few young fellas, and myself. I can remember the first mob we drove in 1951, when we started working with the contractor. We took delivery of about 600 spayed cows at a place called Karntipal, or Chestnut Bore, on Cherrabun station. My brother Barney Lawford was the head stockman at Christmas Creek by then and he brought the cattle across from Cherrabun. They were all Emanuel cattle. From Karntipal we took them across to Piyanpan, the place that the kartiya call Long Hole.

Midday Halt, Kimberley early 20th C.

From there we went to Douglas Yard, which has the Aboriginal name Marrala. And then from there we'd take the mob up to One Tree, which the blackfellas call Yakanarra. There used to be a big delivery camp there, for the three Emanuel properties: Go Go, Christmas Creek and Cherrabun. That's where the stockmen would hand over the cattle, and the manager would hand the delivery note to the drover.

We'd usually take delivery at One Tree, and then cross over the Fitzroy River at a waterhole near Old Cherrabun, which we called Parukupan. Then when we reached the other side of Alexander Island, we'd cross the other river at a place called Liikil. That's a waterhole about two miles south of the Quanbun Downs homestead. Once we had got the mob across the river we had no real worries. We could follow the stock route along the river through Noonkanbah, Liveringa and Mt Anderson, and then on to Derby or Broome.

Anyway, back in 1951 we got a lot of winter rain. Over six inches! It rained almost non-stop and everything we had was soaking wet. We had all those cattle on that Alexander Island and we couldn't move them because of that black soil. When it's wet that black soil becomes very boggy. I think that rain must have lasted for a week. Those two rivers, the Fitzroy and the Cunningham, came up in flood and we were stuck in the middle.

We were stuck on that island for three or four days with 600 cattle, and both rivers running a banka. There was no way we could get them across at Liikil, so we had to go back to where that old Jubilee yard is and swim them across there. Everything we had was soaking wet, swags, overcoats, clothes, everything! We took that mob through the bush, through Warrimbah and the back of Noonkanbah, and then continued on down to Broome. And we didn't lose any of those cattle.

It would take us about four weeks to move a mob of cattle from Go Go to Derby, and about three weeks from Lanji Crossing to Broome. After you cross the river at Lanji you don't have any good camping places because it's too scrubby. So we used to walk the cattle over the usual eight mile a day limit. It would take us about seven weeks altogether to take a mob from Go Go to Broome, and another three weeks to come back with the horses. We would have done about seven trips a year when we were working for the contractor, though I couldn't say how many trips we would have done altogether. We had to be on the road all the time so we didn't get to see our families much.

Droving cattle, 1950s.

As the boss drover, I was getting paid about three pound a week. Out of that I had to buy all my clothes and other gear. But the stockmen who were working with me were getting nothing. Shirt, trousers, hat, boots and a feed were all they'd get. They got no money at all; they wouldn't have known what money looked like.

I'd take possession of the delivery note. You've got to keep it somewhere safe, in your swag or saddle bag, and hand it over when you reach your destination. Either you give it to the drover who takes over from you, or you give it to the stock agent in Derby if you take the mob all the way yourself. In those days the stock agent was a kartiya by the name of Rowell. He would wait until his men had counted the cattle before he'd accept the delivery note. Rowell had a few of his people there with horses, but it was usually us that drove the cattle down onto the boat. After they were loaded we'd head back to the station for the next lot.

In those days some of the stations were running sheep rather than cattle, and we usually had a few problems droving a mob of cattle through those stations. After we crossed Alexander Island at Liikil, we joined the stock route which ran along the river through Quanbun Downs, which was a sheep station. Jeff Rose was the manager of Quanbun back then, and he used to come down and tell us, "I don't want you mob camping here, even if it's wet. You'll bugger up the paddocks. Keep those cattle moving!"

We would have to continue on to Noonkanbah, keeping the cattle on the move all the time. No way could we have a day off! But I used to be a bit cunning, and I wouldn't go through there in one day. I'd stop and camp somewhere. Just as long as we kept the cattle going all the time, doing three or four mile a day. It was good grass there you know, and we had to nurse the cattle along all the way for those eight miles.

Sometimes when we came through Jeff Rose would say, "It'd be better if you camped three or four miles down the track, but don't camp around here." We had to keep moving all the time through that sheep country. Especially when we were passing through Liveringa. The kartiya who was manager there, Kim Rose, was also a hard man. He didn't like drovers going through his sheep paddocks. We couldn't even go off the stock route and down to the river to water our cattle. He made us follow the stock route and water the cattle at the billabongs. But he used to like getting killers from us.

Killer.

This country is feeling very sad

On my last trip droving bullocks we had a thousand head or more. I had seven blokes with me; Chum Lee and a mob of young fellas. Eight people were a lot for a droving camp. We took delivery of those bullocks at Paliyarra (Bloodwood Bore) on Christmas Creek, and we took them right down to Derby. A thousand head! That's a big mob of cattle to drove.

We had a bit of a rush which was caused by a kid the name of Arthur Kylie. He's still alive today. He was standing watch at night, and he must have got hungry and come back to the pack saddle to get a tin of meat. But he opened it around where he was watching the bullocks. And you know what bullocks are like when they're asleep, if they smell something like that. They just go mad! They started singing out, "Barr barr" and they all took off.

1920s open range pasture.

We couldn't make out what had frightened them, so the next morning I went down to see if I could find out. That's when I found the can from the tinned meat. He must have had a feed and just chucked the can on the grass. The bullocks smelt it and took off.

But our first real rush came near to where Looma is now. One of the night horses had a stick poke him in the kurntu, the prick or whatever you call it, and it made him buck. He galloped through the mob, and they took off. We got them all back except for about 60; but we were over-number anyway. We used to pick them up, you know, if another drover had lost some. That's how we ended up with over-number. We used to save them for killer on the road; both for ourselves, and for anybody that came out for some meat.

Old Jack Huddleston, Henry Skinner, and their mob were following one day behind us, and they picked up the bullocks we had lost. We took that mob to Derby for loading into a ship bound for the Philippines. But we had to hold them in Derby for three weeks before the Government decided that they'd allow them to be shipped there. They were the first cattle to be inoculated. Old Emanuel himself was there on the delivery day, and the Philippines mob came out to the yards to buy them.

All of us in the droving camp used to eat the same tucker; which consisted of bread, beef, and tea. The station would supply us with flour for making damper, some tea, salted meat and some tinned meat. Sometimes we'd also get a few tins of jam or some cheese. That's all, nothing else! We would never get any fruit or vegetables. We used to knock over a sheep now and then, when we were going through the sheep country. If our numbers were short then, instead of shooting one of our bullocks, we'd kill a sheep. Or we might kill a kangaroo, a wanyjirri. There were plenty of them around in those days, all along the river. But there aren't many wanyjirri left nowadays, because they've all been poisoned.

Now I want to say something about the equal wage decision. You know in 1967 the courts decided that Aboriginal stockmen should receive equal wages to what the kartiya were getting. Well, that decision did a lot of damage up here; it really disrupted our communities.

At the time of the wage decision there were a lot of people here on Christmas Creek, including a lot of old people. The manager used those old people for work like fencing, cutting posts, and rope making. They were just on rations and such, not on wages. When the equal wage was awarded, Emanuel decided that it was too expensive to keep those old people; too expensive to feed them or give them rations. "They'll have to move off", he said, "we only pay people to work."

Station workers, 1950s.

They picked out about 10 stockmen, a few house girls, and that's all the workers they wanted. All the other people, old people included, had to get off the station. Otherwise they would have been sitting down there starving. Emanuel wouldn't give them any rations; nothing at all.

Most of those people walked into Fitzroy Crossing, to where the Windmill Reserve is. But they had to make a camp on this side of the river for a while to wait for the warrampa, or floodwaters, to subside. Fortunately one of their relations was a missionary worker at Yilak, the Fitzroy Crossing Mission, and he came across in a boat with some supplies.

When the river went down they were able to get across just west of the old bridge, and the same bloke had a truck waiting for them on the other side, which took them down to the Windmill Reserve. (That was Mr Jimmy Bieunderry. He's dead now, but he earned a great deal of respect from the people for his devoted service to them over the years. He deserves recognition, but it's our custom not to speak the name of a dead person around his relatives or those who were close to him.) So the people set up camp at Windmill Reserve, and the mission supplied them with two big hessian bags of flour. After that they just had to wait for assistance from the Government, to wait for welfare aid.

After the owners had got the people to leave the stations, they didn't want them back. Most of them couldn't get a job anywhere! Only when the stations were short of workers would the managers come and get them, and then they only picked out a few. Most of them couldn't even go back to their own place and sit down, because Emanuel didn't like them sitting down and not working. They had to be either stockmen or station hands.

Fred Hansen (Noonkanbah), fractured skull. "You could see his skull. He recovered." Limerick Pindan, Walmajarri women and children. Bough shelter, Australian Inland Mission, Fitzroy Crossing 1940s. Photo Margaret Wells.

They only employed three or four blokes for the fencing work, and they didn't employ very many stockmen. Their wives and kids were allowed to stay there with them; but all the rest of the community, maybe three or four hundred people, had been forced to leave. They were scattered all over the place. Wherever they could find work. That's how they split this community up!

Women station workers and their children, 1950s.

Around that time the Emanuels had a manager call Kevin Norton working for them at Christmas Creek. Now it was the Aboriginal people who taught that bloke how to run the station and how to work cattle; but he didn't have much respect for Aboriginal people and he didn't treat them very well. One day back in mid '79 Kevin Norton and some white stockmen stopped a truckload of Aboriginal stockmen who were returning to the station after a drinking session in Fitzroy Crossing. I wasn't there but they told me that Norton and his stockmen dragged those Aborigines out one by one and punched them around.

That's when Chum Lee, Tuluk and the others walked off the station, and afterwards refused to work for that kartiya. It was on account of that incident. I had been given the sack from Christmas Creek not long before then, and had started doing contract work at Noonkanbah with the Peter Ross mob, so I wasn't directly involved.

The Christmas Creek mob went to see the Department of Community Welfare officer at Fitzroy, a bloke by the name of Stan Davey. He raised the matter with the police. When no action was taken he put it into the hands of the Aboriginal Legal Service. The Emanuels took up Norton's defence and put a lot of lawyers onto the case, all stacked up against Phillip Vincent, who represented the Aboriginal stockmen on behalf of ALS.

I don't know what Norton got out of it, but he won the case. Nonetheless, nearly all of the Christmas Creek mob still refused to work for Norton. That's why, from that day on, until Norton left, you wouldn't see any Aboriginal people working for Christmas Creek station.

Aboriginal station dwellings of the '60s, deserted by mid '70s.

They decided to come back here sometime later. They set up a camp down at Ngumpan until they were granted the excision over that place where the Wangkatjunga community is now. The old men started the move by telling some young fellas that they had to come back here for law business.

Nearly all the Wangkatjunga mob who sat down at Windmill Reserve have come back here now. Even some of the old people have come back to live here. A lot of our people are still living here in Fitzroy Crossing though. They're intermarried now, married into different tribes.

When the basic wage came in, the station ran more or less the same way as before, except that we were short-handed in a lot of areas. Also, Emanuel's policy was to only offer work from March till September and no more. They said that they couldn't pay wages beyond that. We didn't have time to clean the country out properly, and so there were clean-skins everywhere. And then, every different manager that came along had different ideas on how things should be done.

The cattle started to run down, and I think a lot of it was the manager's fault. For instance, we had a paddock with a stud herd of good cows and good bulls, and that just went into decline. After all the Aboriginal people had left, following on from the introduction of the basic wage, there was no thought given to breeding good cattle or having good horses.

There were a lot more horses than those people could handle, so they started killing them off for pet meat. One manager here shot nearly all the breeding stock that we had on the place, mares and foals too! A lot of good horses, working horses and all, were just shot. It made us feel terribly sorry. We knew those horses, we had worked with them over the years. They shot most of the mules too. We're all sorry about that. They were all good working animals.

One thing that I'd say is: they don't have people now who are experienced enough to muster cattle on horseback. There are no blackfellas working on those stations. It's all jackaroo kartiyas, as they call them, whitefellas. They don't know how to muster properly. They don't know the country. They might get lost if you sent them out mustering on horseback. They don't really know much at all. They have to use a helicopter, otherwise they'd get lost and perish in the bush somewhere.

Now I don't like that helicopter mustering. They're killing a lot of cattle doing the mustering that way. They muster them over too great a distance, with the helicopter chasing along behind. Many of the cows lose their calves, and some bullocks are so knocked up from being galloped such a long way, they just lie down and die. That's why the helicopters kill a lot of cattle.

A lot of cattle die after they've been brought into yards too. From stress and heat exhaustion. Just think of all those overheated animals being crowded into the yards during the heat of the day. Sometimes a thousand head would die in the yards. It happens all over: Cherrabun, Christmas Creek, Go Go, and wherever they're using helicopters.

I think that all the stations have gone downhill as a result, every one of them. It makes me sad that not one station runs properly, like they used to. They're all run down. I'll tell you about the place next door, Bohemia Downs, where I was born. There's not a working bore on the whole place. There's still one permanent waterhole and a few cattle drinking around it; but there's been no improvements done in a long time. Nothing at all! It's just been abandoned. You know, the station owners just walked off it.

Kimberley station, early days.

I'm trying to get that place in the whiteman way, and I'm trying to get an excision on it for a start. The Government took the lease off the previous owners, ALCCO (Australian Land and Cattle Company - Ed.), because they hadn't done any improvements. The ownership is all up in the air now, while the Government decides on all this station break-up business. Its just a ghost pastoral lease at the moment.

That's what happens when those millionaires take over the stations; they try to get what they can as quick as they can. My father and a few other people used to make a living out of that place and he wouldn't worry about anything else, as long as he could get the bullocks to the meatworks. He wasn't worried about getting out quick, he would just stop there, look after his cattle, and breed them up. And look after the country as well, maintain all the bores and such.

I still reckon that we should be part of the cattle industry. Us blackfellas from Ngumpan to Ngarantjartu should have a part of this station. We can do it our own way, like the way we've been taught. That's the only thing we know, how to nurse cattle and grow cattle. And how to care for the country, how to burn the right areas at the right time. But kartiya have different ideas and a different way; and the country is feeling very sad as a result.

But I reckon that they should never have driven the Aboriginal people off the stations. At least they should have shown some consideration and provided food for the people who weren't working. Given them a ration or a feed, or killed a bullock for them when necessary. The station owners shouldn't have forced them to leave, because those people were born there and grew up there. Some of them spent all their working lives there, and a lot of their people died there.

And what made it harder was to send them to a place like Fitzroy Crossing. This group here got split up and put into different places, and controlled by people with different ideas. When the drinking rights came in, well, it ruined everything. You could say that those people were made into alcoholics by the treatment they got and the conditions they were forced to live under. But I feel very strongly that they shouldn't have hunted them off the stations in the first place.

Those stations owe these people something; some sort of compensation at least. If a station owner is thinking of selling out, then the Government should offer to buy the station for the Aboriginal people who grew up there and worked there.

On Go Go, early 1940s. Photo Margaret Wells.

CHAPTER 2

In those days you couldn't cry

Jock Shandley

Walmajarri man (1925 -)

Puluku (Bush name)   Jampijin (Skin name)

"You're finished with your mob now."

I started running the camp at Christmas Creek back when George Dean was the station manager. I was living in the Aboriginal camp with my people when George Dean came and picked me out. He was looking at me in the camp and must have decided that I was smart. He told me, "Righto, I'm making you the head stockman, you'll be the boss for this camp." I was only young but I had a team of good working men under me, a very good team of stockmen. In those days we were working for stick tobacco, shirt and trousers, boots and hat, or maybe a pocket knife. This would have been sometime after 1940, though I couldn't tell you the year because I've never been to school.

Brooking Springs sheep yards with the Napier Range as rear fence.

Windmill and tank on Leopold Downs.

When it was time to start mustering, George Dean would come down to the camp, call me out and say, "Righto, grease your pack saddle and riding saddle, and get all the boys doing it too. Get all your plant ready." Right, so I'd go and hound the stockmen. Tell them to get their saddles greased with bullock fat, and to get everything ready for mounting. The next day we'd go out to the big stock paddock on the river, which we called Shoela Yard. We'd get all the horses into the horse yard, and we'd draft all the workers out that day. That took two days, one to pack the saddles and one to get the horses. Right, on the third day we'd get the trailer ready and bring it to the front of the store, and the manager would come down with the key and supervise the loading of supplies.

The next day, the fourth day, the manager would tell me to go up to Shoela Yard and start mustering from there. The blackfella name for that place is Pitipa. We used to get into that wild country around MacDonald, Saul's Creek and Camel Rockhole, and get all the scrubbers rounded up. We'd bring them in and brand them; and we'd keep mustering and branding cattle from around there. We used to sort the bullocks out and bring them back in little groups to the big bullock paddock. That's Pinnacle Paddock, or Six Mile, where Chum Lee and his group have their excision now. We'd keep on mustering and branding until we had whatever number they wanted for the ship, usually five or six hundred.

When we had got together the number of bullocks needed for the road, George Dean would tell me, "Righto, take these down to One Tree." So we started out from Christmas Creek with the bullocks. On the first night we used to camp either at Dusty Yard or somewhere around Paliyarra. From there we'd take them to Spinifex Yard and then on to Chestnut, Long Hole and Douglas Yard before getting to One Tree. In those days there weren't any yards, so we'd have to watch them with the night horses. We'd keep them out in the open; we'd never try to jam them up.

Righto, we knew that old Ted Millard was going to come down there the next morning. He was the big general for all the Emanuel stations. He'd get on a horse with his pipe smoking away, and ride out into the middle of the bullocks. He always used to smoke that pipe, old Ted Millard. He'd go in and pick out the cattle he wanted to send on the road to Derby. I wasn't droving in those days, I was the head stockman for Christmas Creek. The drover was a kartiya from Queensland, old Percy William. He was a real drover too. So Percy William would come down from Go Go and we'd hand the cattle over to him.

There were five people working with old Percy, three kartiya and two blackfellas. He always had a whiteman as cook and two white stockmen. Old Percy was the head drover. He'd have one Aborigine up front working with the bullocks and one Aboriginal horse tailer. In those days, when we first started, they weren't allowed to have more than two Aborigines in a droving plant. But Percy would always have three kartiya with him, always. The cook would follow along behind the horses driving the little cart, the sulky or whatever you call it. You know, the type with only two wheels.

Early mustering plant in a Kimberley riverbed.

Patrick Echo, Jimbo Johnson, Johnny Echo.

Johnny Malay with horning shears, Patrick Echo.

Desmond Bedford.

Now in my time, when I started droving, I used to have five or six stockmen with me because I was droving more cattle. The biggest mob I ever took was a thousand head. I had to split that mob and drove them in two groups, otherwise we couldn't feed them. No way in the world! They'd spread out too much if we kept them in one mob, so we had two mobs, separated by about a mile. Before sundown each day we used to bring them back together, box them up and camp them. Oh brother! Droving a thousand head of cattle was too much trouble. Just as well they didn't rush on me or we really would have been in trouble.

Anyway, as I was saying, we used to hand the cattle over to Percy William and head back to Christmas Creek with the plant the following morning. We might get one or two nights' spell, and then we'd be into it again. We'd get stuck into branding calves until it was time to send off some more bullocks. Usually we'd send off five or six mobs a year.

When I first started out as head stockman they let me live in the camp with the other Aborigines, but after a couple of years they took me out of the Aboriginal camp. The manager came down and said, "You're finished with your mob. From now on you camp with us, and eat at the table with us." This fella George Dean wasn't a bad man; in fact he was a little bit good. But all the same, the Aboriginal workers didn't get any pay in those days. It really was a very, very hard life. But still it was a good life. People were happy in the camp, not like nowadays!

Today, it doesn't matter if you go into the town in the day or in the night, you're bound to run into trouble with the drunks. And it's hard to get workers because they've all been spoilt with grog and sit-down money. That's nowadays. But back then it was a good life, especially when we got away from the station and out into the bush for the mustering and branding. It'd be hard work right enough, but we had a lot of fun too. We used to be really happy out in the bush.

Justine Brown with grandson Emmanuel and Munmurria Andrews.

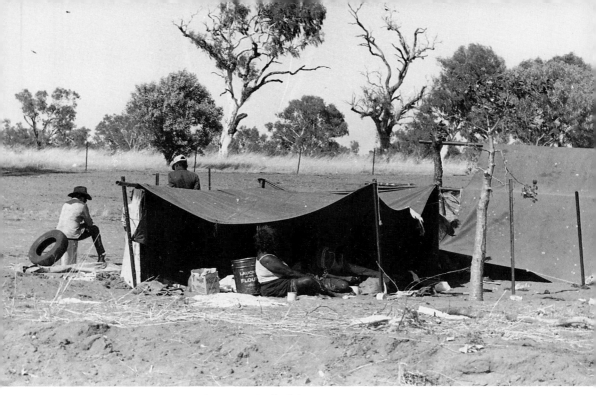

George Brooking, Alice Gardiner, a stockcamp near Noonkanbah.

After I had been running the camp at Christmas Creek for a few years, Go Go started looking around for a head stockman. So they decided to move me to here. It's a big place Go Go, it's the main cattle station around here. It was also a very busy station. Cherrabun and Christmas Creek used to knock off a bit earlier, but Go Go used to keep going and going and going. So they moved me to Go Go, and I ran the place for more than 20 years. I was head stockman here right up until I went into the police force.

That would have been around 1973. I was the first police aide in Fitzroy Crossing. I remember I was working out in the bull paddock when the police came out to see me. I had only just jumped down from the saddle, and two of the Fitzroy Crossing policemen came up to me and said, "You've got to go into the police force now." They must have already talked with the manager and cleared it with him. So I was sort of drafted into the police force. I was in the police force for nine years and it's about four or five years now since I left.

We used to mother them up properly

When I was sent to run things at Go Go, I started wondering how I was to keep such a big station going. So I organised things the same way as I did at Christmas Creek. I'd get all the saddles greased up the first day, and then on the second day I'd go out with some stockmen and we'd muster the horses and draft out all the workers. The following day we'd take the mule cart up to the store and load it up with tucker. The manager of Go Go when I first started was old Ted Millard. He would send us up to Louisa Yard straight after the wet. That's on the station boundary, up near the top end of the Black Hills. Oh, it was hard times boy! Shoeing those horses. In that country you've got to shoe all the horses. We even had to knock down the young horses and shoe them too.

We still weren't getting paid. I even had some kartiya working under me. I'd tell them where to go and what to do. But they were getting paid, and all us Aborigines were getting nothing. Just rations.

Patrick Echo, Johnny Malay.

Expanses of overgrazed, depleted understory, Fitzroy plains.

Johnny Echo gets a stray on Mt Barnett.

They used to send me out to get 700 bullocks in three or four days. Go Go wasn't like Christmas Creek, where you had to look around a bit. On Go Go you could go out and get four or five hundred bullocks in two days. But that was in those days; you couldn't do that now! There's not so many cattle around now.

We'd get up at about three o'clock in the morning, and we'd be on our horses as soon as it became daylight. We'd muster the cattle and bring them back into the cattle camp by about eight or nine o'clock. Then I used to tell the stockmen, "Hurry up and have your dinner, it's cooked there ready for you. We need to hurry because we've got to work a big mob of cattle today." They used to have their dinner, get straight back into their saddles and head out onto the flat to start drafting. There were no yards in those days, so we used to find a good flat and take the cattle there.

If we had time while we were drafting out the bullocks, we'd try to brand as many of the clean-skins as we could. There might be 30 riders that day. I'd put some of them out to hold the cattle, and get four blokes to make a branding fire on the flat. I'd tie a bronco hook

42

up in a tree with a bit of strap, and we'd pick out three or four bronco horses.

They were especially trained for the work. They had to be a big-boned animal too, a semi-draft horse or a mule. They're trained by pulling a weight around the yard first, a bag of sand or a light animal. Then they're trained to handle the weight of a bullock on the end of the rope. A good bronco horse knows his job. Once he takes up the weight you just give him his head. You can't tell him where to go.

So, those stockmen would get on their horses and go out amongst the cattle. If they saw a calf with no brand, they'd rope it and bring it back to the tree. The blokes on the ground would grab it round the hind legs and knock it down, brand it and ear-mark it. Then they'd let it go and wait for another one to be brought up to them. There were four or five men working on the ground, and another mob in their saddles. They used to lasso calves just like you see cowboys do. We'd bronco them in the open in those days.

It didn't matter if we didn't finish them. If we could get half of them done that day, it would give us half a day for other work. If you chase animals around too much on the open flat you stir up the mob too much and it takes a long time to settle them down. It would be getting too late by three or four o'clock, so we'd finish off the branding. We had bullocks to watch. It didn't matter because the calves would come back the next time; they'd come back after the bullocks. You've got to hang onto those bullocks! But we wouldn't just let the cows and calves go, we'd settle them down first. We'd walk them down to the billabong, steady them down and mother them up properly. You have to let all the cattle mill around together, so that the cows can find their calves.

We'd never just gallop them out like they do today with the helicopter. We'd mother them up, let them go, and then those stockmen could go back to the camp. I'd have another mob of stockmen tailing the bullocks while all that was going on, and we always had two horse tailers looking after the horses. They'd have about 30 or 40 head of horses to look after, which had to be watered and hobbled out.

Horse muster, Leopold Downs.

Desmond Bedford, Jimmy Olfin, Mt Barnett.

Windjana Gorge. Napier Range.

Desmond Bedford, Alec Unengen, Patrick Echo, Jeffrey Dutchie.

After we finished the branding, I'd go back to get everything organised in the camp. Such as telling the cook to hurry up and get the 'killer', and telling the men which night horses I wanted made ready. We'd have six night horses, but only two people would do the watch. The other horses would be tied up, prepared ready in case something happened, such as the bullocks stampeding. You know, taking off in the middle of the night. If they took off you'd have to take off with them and try to wheel them back. There were no yards or night paddocks like today, sonny. It's a lot of fun today! This mob have a long spell these days; they put the bullocks into the horse paddock and go into town. In those days, no mate, you wouldn't do that!

Usually, we'd take two or three hour watches. The first watch would be in their saddles and out with the bullocks by six o'clock, and would come off at nine o'clock. They would call out the second mob who would have been having a bit of a sleep. One bloke would go and tell them to put their boots on and get ready while the other one remained in the saddle.

Patrick Norgoodah, Noonkanbah.

Johnny Malay, Jimbo Johnson, Jimmy Echo, Patrick Echo.

Southern Kimberley.

The second lot were on watch till eleven o'clock and then they'd call the third watch, and so on. It all depended on how many men we had. If we were short of men then we'd do a longer watch, which would make us all tired. But if we had plenty of men then we would only go out for one or two hours. The horse tailers used to be the first to go on watch. And the blokes who came into the camp last would be the last in line to do the watch.

So, after we had mustered the first lot of bullocks, we used to bring them all the way down from the top, past Eight Mile and past Go Go homestead. We used to take them down to the same delivery camp at One Tree. When we went past the station, the manager would come down in his motorcar and tell us, "I'll be down there tomorrow." The whiteman drover always used to follow us down to One Tree with his droving plant.

All right, we'd get rid of that mob and then we'd have to get going from there in a hurry because we'd have to muster another mob. We'd go down to the other side, the Douglas side, and get another five or six hundred. There were a lot of bullocks in those days, I'll tell you, half of 'em were bullocks. So we'd be into it again; we didn't get a chance to come back to the station and we didn't get a spell.

There were no Sundays in those days! No, on Sunday we'd be branding. This place now is just like a holiday camp. That's what I'd call it. I'll tell you, this mob working the place today don't even go out on a horse. I see them every morning flying over with two helicopters and an aeroplane to bring the cattle into the yards. This morning there were two planes going over there. I really feel sorry for the cattle, really sorry!

So, we'd rush off the first two lots of bullocks, and then the manager would come and tell us that we could have a break to spell the horses. Then boy, we used to get a rest for five, six or seven days. Something like that. A good spell! Not at the station though; we'd stop near Jiljiyarti Billabong, or somewhere around there. We'd get a chance to wash our clothes and saddle cloths. If somebody's horse was crippled we'd gallop around and get a fresh horse. You know, sometimes horses get a sore back and such. We used to get fresh horses and make up a new plant. Then the manager would come out and say, "Tomorrow I want you to go down to the big dam and do the branding there."

So, we would settle into the branding. But whenever anyone rang up from Perth with an order the manager would race out in the motorcar and say, "Righto, I want another 700 bullocks by the end of the week." We used to be going flat out to get those 700.

What we did in those days was to get the first lot of cattle and make them into coaches. We used to round them up as soon as they galloped away from the place where they were feeding. There might be just 20 or 30. We'd get into them straight away, round them up and hold them for a while. We learnt to do it that way, to hold on to them and make them into coaches. You know, tame them a bit so they're a quiet herd. Then we would walk those cattle along, a bloke at the front, one at each side and one on the tail. Walk them nice and slowly. As soon as we saw another mob of cattle, we would round them up and run them into the coaches. We'd build that little mob up till there was a thousand or thereabouts.

Loading cattle; trucking replaces droving. Harry Scrivener, Manager Old Cherrubin station, in dark shirt.   (Facing:) Malachi Hobbs.

"Follow my arm in."

One thing that we did a lot of in the old days was spaying. The fella that taught me how to spay was Vic Jones. He taught me that down at MacDonald Yard, or Ngalkajirri as the Aboriginal people call it. That's at the back of Christmas Creek, this side of Kurlku. We put one big cow in the crush and he grabbed his knife and said, "Wash your hands and come up with me." Now, say that the cow was standing here... well he opened it up on this side, in front of the rib. He punched two holes in that cow's hip. Then he put his hand in one hole, and told me to put my hand in the other. "Righto," he said, "follow my arm in."

So I followed his arm in right up to the end of his finger. "Do you feel it there, those two ovaries?" he said. "Yeah boss, I got them," I said. He wasn't actually the boss, he was the head stockman then. Right, he gave me the spaying hook and I cut one ovary off and pulled it out; then I cut the one off the other side and pulled that out. "Right, you sew her up," he said. That's the place where I learnt how to do that job - Ngalkajirri.

Boy, that man taught me a lot. He taught me how to cut foals and horses too. Vic Jones and old Ted taught me. I used to do all the branding myself in the days when I was head stockman at Go Go. I used to cut their horses and brand their foals. You wouldn't believe the big mob of foals we branded on Go Go once - 500 foals! That was the biggest lot of branding I ever did, and it took a really long time. Oh, my back was so sore from bending down! My back felt like it had been hit with an axe handle! You know how you have to bend down? It's different to doing cattle you know; you can't lean on foals like you do with calves.

Now, when you're cutting horses you don't do it with them standing up, you've got to knock them down to the ground. You get one of the stockmen to rope him in the yard, and as soon as they've got a head-rope on him, the others pull him from the outside. Then they chuck a leg-rope on him and knock him down.

But you always have to get a good man on his head. You don't knock him down like you would a calf; you've got to grab his head and bring him down slowly. That's the most important part. A horse has a heavy head but a skinny neck. Unless you know how to land the horse's head properly you can easily snap his neck. So then you've got him down on the ground. With a big horse, you've got to tie the leg-ropes to a post and stretch out his legs. With a little foal you only have to loin-rope him, and tie his legs up tight.

Now you always cut a horse with your left hand. You grab his balls with your right hand, and use your left hand to cut him. You see, that way if he kicks out you can't cut his guts open. If you have the knife in your right hand and he starts kicking, you'll let his guts out or you'll injure one of your off-siders. And you always cut it away from you. That way if he starts kicking he will always kick the knife out of your hand.

Stock horses, Moola Bulla 1910-18.

When the stock camp closed down for the year, we would put all the stock camp gear inside the saddle room, and we'd have a spell for a while. Then the manager would come up and say, "I want you to get the tractor and take a big mob of boys out to cut some rails." There were no chainsaws in those days, so we'd have to use axes and cross-cut saw. You know those double handled saws? You get two men pulling on it, just like two monkeys. Ha ha!

Before the tractor came we used to get a lot of mules and hitch them up to a big trailer. One of those ones with two wheels. They used to build them here in the old days, back in the time of those managers. Otherwise we'd use a donkey wagon. We never drove the donkey wagon; an old kartiya bloke used to come up with us. A mob of stockmen would go with the wagon to cut the rails and bring them to the site where the manager wanted the yard built. While that was going on we would start digging with a crowbar and a shovel. That's all we had: a crowbar, shovel, brace-and-bit, adze, axe, cross-cut saw and Number 8 wire. Now, today they would use a chainsaw.

Do you know what's wrong with the chainsaw? I'll tell you. You take three good workers like you had before, you know good axemen. Right, I've got the chainsaw, or maybe he's got it. It only takes one man to do the cutting and the other two just stand by and watch. "Good one! It's going quick," you might say, "chainsaws are better." But it makes the other two workers lazy. They can get away with not doing any work, and so they reckon that chainsaws are good. In the end it does those other two out of a job. I reckon that chainsaws have buggered things up. Yeah, and the power drill too. Those workers would say, "Look at it! It's going quick. Here, you do it and I'll go and put the billy on."

So one man is doing the work and the others are just bludging. They're bringing in a really easy way now. I remember them saying, "We're going to have a lot of easy things now. Don't think about those early days. That's all finished now!" Those axes and things were just for us blackfellas, I think.

Cattle yard and stockhands, Go Go July 1957.

But a lot of good yards were built by hand. Do you see that bull paddock over there? That's the last one that I built. Me and an old kartiya named Fred Spink built that. He's dead now. We also built those five big wooden drafting yards on Go Go. When Fred was putting up those yards, I used to go and give him a hand. Then he went up to Darwin and left the job half finished, so I had to finish it off. Now you have a look at this bull paddock here. When that wood starts to go, they'll peg it out and get a welder to make the new one. That's another easy job! All steel. And now they've got these new portable yards.

This boy of mine knows about them; he works with those portable yards. He was out trapping bulls this year and I went over there to watch him. He moved one this way, and one that way, and made a gate. It's just a one man job with these portable yards. I reckon they're a good thing. You can build a big portable yard in one day. I saw a bloke doing it on his own. He'd just stand it up and bolt it on. They're only light, you know, it isn't hard to carry them. One bloke can do it in a day. Where do you reckon the other mob would be? They'd be down at the pub, I reckon!

Early Noonkanbah station.

I didn't understand what it was all about

Remember I told you how they took me away from the Aboriginal camp and put me in the quarters, living with the white people? Well, after I had gone to Go Go, this young single woman from the camp there started trying to get hitched up with me. After our first night together she wouldn't let go; she started coming to the quarters every night. Some other women would come up with her and they would split off as soon as they got to the quarters. There were about seven or eight whitemen sharing those quarters with me. My woman would come to my room and the other lot might go to another room. I didn't see them, I was only watching mine.

But I felt a bit funny about it with all the kartiya around. In those days we were like dingoes - as soon as we'd see a whiteman we'd sort of hide from him. We were frightened of the whiteman because they were too hard on us in those days. They used to shoot if anything was wrong. They'd shoot you straight away, you know. They were doing that before my time, but the old people used to tell us about it.

They killed a lot of Aborigines in these hills here. They shot them down like dogs! There's a big mob of Aboriginal people buried on the Margaret River. You can see their bones there today, inside a cave. So in those days we Aborigines were frightened of being in the

56

Port Hedland Depot, Native Affairs Dept., 1931.

whiteman's quarters. Really frightened! I was afraid that I might get hunted out, or get a bullet, or anything.

Right, so I told this woman, "You'd better not come back around the kartiya anymore. I'm new here and I'm a bit frightened. You're coming into the quarters too often." I spoke to the manager that morning and said that I was trying to get rid of that woman. But the manager turned around and said, "Well, don't hunt her out. If she wants you, then keep her. I'll give you a saddle for her, and you can take her mustering and branding. You can take her wherever you go." So the manager gave me a saddle and I picked out a quiet horse for her. When I started out from the station with the next big mustering plant, she was on her horse with me. After that she was with me all the time, wherever I went. I suppose that I got a bit tame after the manager said I could have that woman. I felt that the manager was behind me, helping me.

Then, after the first muster, they told me to marry her. The manager made me have that woman and then he said I should marry her properly and finish the job. We were the first Aborigines in this area to get married in the kartiya way. When I got married I was 30 and she was 25, and we're still together here today.

Rita Shandley.

The Fitzroy Crossing Mission was new then; it had only been
there for one year. Mr Bruce Smoker was the minister there. And
another one, Preston Walker, was there. I still know Bruce, I think
he's in Perth now. Anyway, the station manager ran us down there
for the wedding at eight o'clock in the morning. There must have
been a hundred Aboriginal people there, and only three kartiya,
Preston Walker, Bruce Smoker and his wife. I didn't know anything
about this wedding business; it's the kartiya way. Our people just
used to live together "married up" and that was it, they were married.
In the blackfella way that was all there was to it. As long as you had
the woman walking with you, you were married. That's what we call
a kangaroo marriage. But Rita and I were the first Aborigines
around here to get married according to the kartiya way. I've still got
the marriage certificate; I'll dig it out for you later.

MARRIAGES IN THE ...WEST KIMBERLEY... REGISTRY DISTRICT

Column.			
1.	No. 2/55 Registered on the 26 Jan 1955 by G T MORRIS , District Registrar		
2.	When and Where Married	1955 22nd January United Aborigines Mission Church Fitzroy Crossing WA	
3.	Christian Name and Surname of the Parties	Jock Shandley	Rita Bell
4.	Age ... years	30	25
5.	Condition of the Parties ... (Bachelor, Widower or Divorcee; Spinster, Widow or Divorcee.)	Bachelor	Spinster
6.	Rank or Profession or Occupation	Head Stockman	House-keeper
7.	Place and Country of Birth	Gogo Station, W A	Cherrabun Station W A

Anyway, when we got there at eight o'clock they had already started the church service. I didn't know anything about church; I didn't understand what it was all about. All the people there were dressed up and they were having a sing-song for our wedding. We sat down in the chairs up the front, and Preston Walker stood up and started talking for us. I still remember him saying, "I'm going to marry you two today. Now you're going to be properly married, husband and wife, the whiteman way." I didn't know it, but he had two rings with him. Preston Walker gave me one ring and said, "Put it on her finger." So I put it on her finger and then I pulled it off again; and then I put it back on her finger. I was sort of pulling it back and forth. But in the end I put it on her finger and left it there. I've still got my ring but I think Rita has lost hers; it's probably on the ground around here somewhere.

After the wedding was finished we came back to the station, and all the managers shook my hand for getting married. Then a few days later they loaded me up with tucker and sent me over to the big dam. They wanted me to look after that paddock during the wet, just in case somebody came around the back way. I had to stay there; but I was pleased about that. It was a really good life out there on our own. But we weren't really on our own, because a big mob of people followed us out there. People who wanted to walkabout out in the open, hunting goanna and such. They wanted to stay out there as well. That was no problem, because there was plenty of killer out there. I had a saddle and everything, so as soon as the salt meat ran out, we used to go out with the horses and get a killer. I used to start work from out there too, and ride in to the station to get the plant and stockmen organised.

Now, I'm the first Aborigine around here that got two things: married, and 'the wheel'. Ted Millard had one of those short wheel base Land Rovers, and I asked him if I could buy it. I was on wages by that time. They had started me off on five pound a week, which was good money for those days. ($10 in present currency, indexed for inflation, $60 in 1988 - Ed.) It was the same as Percy William and the other drovers were getting. Only the top men got that sort of money. But jeez, I couldn't buy a bloody hat for that today! This one I've got on would be about $30 nowadays, or it might be even more. It goes up every day. You go to the shop and look at the price on the top of a bottle of tomato sauce, or anything. Everything keeps going up and up in price. What are we going to do? We may as well go without.

Anyway, I had been saving all my money from mustering, and I had about 200 pounds in the station safe. When I asked Ted Millard about buying the car, he said: "Yeah, I'll sell it to you." So I got the first 'wheel', and everyone was watching me as I drove it around.

Got up ready to go to the races. John Wells (child in the cab), unknown, Nosey Paddy (split septimum), Roslyn Willie, Oobagooma man (in hat), Dora, children unknown, Freddie Marker (in hat), (trailer:) Frank, Eileen Yandaman, Tony, (first head on right of rail). Photo Margaret Wells.

Meda, in front of the old kitchen, 1950s. Some from Oobagooma, some from Sunday Island, coming in now and again for a feed. Unknown, Alice Lennard, Maudie Lennard, Biddy, Roslyn Lennard, Eileen Yandaman, three unknown, Freddie Marker, unknown, Frank. Photo Margaret Wells.

They were getting around on foot, and there I was with a motorcar. And I'm still driving around today.

But, for most of my time working as head stockman I got no wages at all. I just got rations like all the other stockmen. Everyone from the stock camp got the same issue at the start of the season: one shirt, one pair of trousers, boots and a hat. Sometimes we'd get a plug of tobacco as well. We were also given a swag and blanket each, but they had to last a few years.

When we had finished the mustering for the year, the manager would come and tell the stockmen, "You fellas can go on holiday tomorrow, for the wet season. Bring all your gear in, saddles and everything." They would take all the stock camp gear up, all the saddles and things, and put it all in the saddle room. Some of them would even take their swag up, if they didn't want it with them during the holidays. They would put it in the store and tell the boss, "That's my swag beneath there." Not everyone did that; some of them wanted to keep their swags with them wherever they were staying.

The boss would get all the stockmen up from the camp and line them up in front of the store. He'd have a bit of paper with a list of those men to let go on holiday that day. They'd all be waiting there, and he'd call out, "Righto Peter, bring your tucker bag." Peter would walk out, and the boss would say, "Get your rations for the holidays". Then he'd call out the next one. They'd all be standing there really quiet, listening. There was none of this coming in and out of the store. Only whitemen were allowed inside the store; the blackfellas had to stay outside.

The boss would only send half the workers off on their holidays at first, and keep the other half to do some work around the station. Before they went off he would tell them, "You can go for three weeks. After three weeks you've got to come back to work." "All right boss", they'd say, and they would take off for Cherrabun or somewhere. They'd go off to a corroboree or that sort of thing. They would walk to wherever they were going, and carry their swag if they had it with them. And when they came back, the other mob would go on their holidays. The boss used to work them just like they'd work horses. There was no government protection and the managers could do what they wanted. The blackfellow was treated the same as a horse! All the stations were issued with some sort of permit to work Aborigines. But there were good times as well, and a lot of good aspects to the station life.

Thomas Skinner (below), and spectators (facing); Noonkanbah rodeo 1986.

"He got rifle."

My father was a bullocky, a kartiya by the name of Jim Shandley. When he first came to Fitzroy he was carting supplies to the stations with a bullock team. When he didn't have a load he would stop and do some work for the station manager, firstly at Go Go and then at Fossil Downs. He worked for Willie MacDonald, not Bill MacDonald but his old father Willie. And he worked for a few others too. I heard a few stories about him from Dick Fellon, who used to be the owner of the Fitzroy Crossing pub. Dick knew him because he used to drink at the bar in his spare time.

Apparently he was a real fighting man. If anyone picked him he wouldn't just go for one bloke, he'd go for three. He'd take them out on the flat and really give it to them. One man wasn't a match for him, he'd mince him up, he'd almost kill him. I don't know why he was like that, but he must have been a really tough old bloke. A real fighter. I don't know how big he was because I've never seen him. He must have just filled my old woman up and taken off. One of them blokes, a dingo!

I didn't know anything about him until I got to be about 10, and I started to understand things. Before then they used to tell me that my father was a whiteman but I didn't ever take any notice. I hadn't yet realised what colour my skin was. But when I grew up a bit, I noticed that the other fellas had darker skin than me. It was then that those old blokes, Ted Millard, Dick Fellon and the others, told me, "Well, your father was a whiteman. He came from Scotland and his name was Jim Shandley." From what I hear he's pegged out down at Marble Bar. That mob down there know where his grave is; they say it's on the bank of the river at Marble Bar.

I don't properly know where Marble Bar is, I've never been past Port Hedland. I don't even know what the country is like down that way. But my kids would know because they've been all around the place. I've never been down to Roebourne or Carnarvon and I've never been up to Darwin. I've only been as far east as Wyndham and Kununurra. So you see I've spent all my life in the Kimberley.

Bullocks hauling wool dray, Noonkanbah early 20th C.

In those early days, relations were not very good between the Aborigine and the whiteman. You know, they really were no good! I remember at Go Go station, the manager and his mob used to come out onto the lawn every afternoon after tea. They'd sit down and have a yarn. But they could also hear what was going on down at the Aboriginal camp. If anyone was making a noise, or if a bit of fighting was going on, or kids crying, you'd hear the manager shout, "Shut up!" Then if you didn't shut up, you'd see him coming down. He'd walk up to the camp and say, "Shut that kid up!" or "Shut that woman up!" Whoever was crying. That was really hard in those days, you couldn't even make a noise. That's the way the whiteman used to keep the place quiet.

In those days too, the kartiya used to give Aboriginal men a flogging. Or they'd lock them up in the store or somewhere. It was the manager who used to flog them. Then, from those days, the blackfella got more and more frightened of the whiteman. If anyone in the camp made a noise or started crying, another blackfella would tell them, "Sssh, don't cry! Kartiya might come! He got rifle!" I still remember all that. You couldn't make a noise, couldn't cry, couldn't have any dogs barking. If any of the camp dogs barked through the night, the manager or the police would come down with a gun the next day and blow their heads in. They'd shoot the fucking lot!

Splinter

I'll tell you a story about a bloke called Splinter. He was a really good stockman. He was riding horses when I was only a kid, and I used to watch him sometimes. Now, Ted Millard would send Splinter on the road droving bullocks. But Splinter only used to go half way. He'd go to Cherrabun, to the delivery camp at One Tree perhaps, and then he'd turn around and come back. He didn't want to go droving, so he'd run away from the droving camp and come back to Go Go. When he did, the house girl would go and see the manager on her way to work, and tell him, "That boy is back here again." He used to ask, "Oh, is Splinter back? Well, tell him to stay there." The manager used to have a talk with Splinter and then put him on the job again. He didn't give him a flogging; he'd just put him on again, and make him work around the station. He was giving him time.

Then when another mob of bullocks were ready to go on the road, they'd send Splinter again. But the same thing would happen. He might have gone as far as Quanbun or Noonkanbah, but he'd run away and come back to Go Go. I don't know how many times he did that, I was only a kid at the time. But I was a big kid, so I knew what was happening. I think that Splinter's problem was that he had a young woman. Maybe he used to come back every time to be with the young gin he had in the camp. I think that's why he didn't want to go droving. He was afraid somebody might get that woman.

Anyway, the manager must have got a gutful of him one day. So, the last time that he ran away, they went out and caught him. I think this is how it happened. Vic Watkin was managing Cherrabun back then, a Queenslander. Bert Smith was manager at Christmas Creek and Bert Lawford manager at Bohemia Downs. Lawford was cruel, really hard that one. I reckon that Ted Millard must have talked to those three about Splinter. Because he kept running away, he had become a bad influence on the other stockmen. It looked as if he didn't like the job. Someone must have arranged for those managers from Cherrabun, Christmas Creek and Bohemia Downs to meet Ted Millard at Number 2 Bore on Go Go.

Violet Valley pastoral station, 1940s.

Violet Valley, 1930s.

There was a borer there at the time, sinking that Number 2 Bore. It might have been Billy McCaven. When Splinter ran away this last time he didn't go back to the station, but set his camp up over on the Number 2 Hill. At the time Joe Wampi's father, old man Limestone Billy, was working with the borer, helping that kartiya put the bore down. Splinter used to walk in every night to the borer's camp to get some tea and tobacco from Limestone Billy.

Now, those four managers – Ted Millard, Vic Watkin, Bert Smith and Bert Lawford – all arrived at Number 2 Bore on the same day. They told Joe Wampi's father, "When he come up, that boy, in the night, you make him big fire... make a fire so we'll know he's there. We gotta hide..." They didn't want Splinter to know that they were there or he might run away. That's why they told the old fella to make his fire out a bit from the borer's camp. Their plan was to wait till Splinter was at the fire, and then to surround it and capture him. They really wanted him by then. What they wanted him for I don't know, but I know what happened to him!

They also told the old man to make a lot of noise so that they could tell where he was. When Splinter came up that night to get some tea and tobacco, old Limestone Billy did as the kartiya had asked. He built up the fire, made some tea and started asking questions so that the kartiya could pick where they were. The four managers came up from different directions and grabbed Splinter, and chained him up for the night. I guess they would have used a donkey chain for that. They were ready to finish him off then.

Maybe one of them killed him early the next morning or maybe waited till later, but they got him. His bones are still there. Last year my daughters went walking up there on the hill looking for fruit, and they came across those bones. That's on Number 2 Hill, the big outcrop of limestone on your left if you're going to Christmas Creek from here. That's where Splinter's bones are.

Those managers wanted to get rid of Splinter because he was spoiling the young fellas. He was a good stockman but he was a bad influence. They caught him out there and someone blew him out. I don't know why four managers came for just one fella. I suppose they must have got together and decided that it was time. Bert Lawford was the hardest of them and he killed a few people on Bohemia. After the manager got back to the station some of the stockmen asked him what he had done with Splinter. He told them, "Oh, I sent him to Halls Creek. He's no good here, so he's gone to Halls Creek with a letter." But he was lying to those Aborigines. Splinter hadn't been sent to Halls Creek, he was dead.

Now in those days, following the first storm, the manager used to send someone out with some pack-horses full of tucker. They would ride around the country and find out where the rain had fallen. You know, so that they could come back and tell the manager, "Boss that Long Hole is full of water from the first rain, and that big dam too. There's plenty of water and plenty of green feed over that way; but it's all dry west of there." Something like that.

Well that year they sent out an old bloke named Saturday, a good stockman. He was riding around as the manager told him to, having a proper look around with his offsider, when he saw this one track of a motorcar. Saturday was a brainy bloke; he worked with me and I got to know him well. He's gone now unfortunately. Anyway, he was alongside Number 2 Hill and he ran into the smell of something dead. "Something smelling here, you hang on the horses here." He followed the smell and he went up on the hill and had a look in all those big holes, and came across Splinter's body.

After he had finished his job for the manager, he went back to the Aboriginal camp and told the mob, "Don't you fellas cry, but that man is dead, he's finished, they shot him!" In those days you couldn't cry or the manager would come straight down and demand to know why you were crying. They cried quietly all right. That's how they found out he was dead, that he had been shot.

In those days, if any Aborigines saw a station man riding anywhere near the camp they'd sing out, "kartiya, kartiya coming! Sssh, hold that dog. Quick, hold him! Whitefella coming! Whitefella!" They used to frightened us, because whiteman have killed too many Aboriginal people in this country. Aboriginal people were frightened because they had nobody behind them, nobody to help them. Now today, there's the Government watching, kartiya can't do those sort of things anymore. We're all together now. They can't do anything like that.

North-west station workers early 1920s.

Like policemen, those station managers

I remember when my mother and stepfather took me out of the camp and we ran away from the station. I was only a kid, so I had to go where my parents went. But I didn't mind. My stepfather decided to run away because something was wrong with the boss, a bad mood or something. We lived out in the bush for something like a year, we used to hide out in those big hills over there. The old woman would go digging in the creek bed every day for some yams or whatever she could find, and my stepfather went out hunting for bush tucker. He was good with a spear, he'd get any sort of kangaroo, emus, goannas, all sorts of things. Just with a spear, no rifle.

In the end they got the police on us. The police were based in Fitzroy Crossing, and the managers used to get them to look for anyone who had run away from the station. They found out the name of the waterhole where we had gone to live from one of the stockmen. The manager would have asked, "Where's that old man?" And somebody would have said, "He's living in those hills over there," and given the name of the waterhole where we were living.

Right, the police came out and grabbed my old man, chained him up, and walked him back to the station. Back in those days they used neck chains, they slung the chain around the prisoner's neck. They chained him, took him back to the station, tied him up, and gave him a good flogging. They used to use a pick handle, axe handle, or whatever they could pick up. They really belted that old man! I don't know what was in the manager's mind. Maybe he was trying to teach him not to run away again. But boy, they kicked the guts out of him!

And then they put him back to work. They put him onto cutting the wood; and the manager used to watch from the house to see if he was still working. Poor bloody bloke, he was really sweating.

The whiteman used to come to this place and belt the Aborigine; tie him up and belt him. I used to see them do it when I was a kid. They wouldn't touch you if you were a kid or a woman. They would only belt the men. That's because the man was the leader, he was the one taking his family away from the station. Usually the police would pick them up, but if the police were somewhere else then the manager would ride out with a pack-horse and get them. They were like policemen, those station managers. He would chain them with a donkey chain and a padlock. Take them in, tie them up the same way, and flog them. They didn't go free. No way in the world!

My old man, the Aboriginal one who married my mother, what I call the proper one, is pegged not far from here. His grave is out on Gap Hill. Do you know the Gap Creek sign out along the highway towards Halls Creek? Well, up along that creek up in the hills, that's where my old man is pegged out. My stepfather.

I'll tell you another thing that I remember about those early times. You see, I was born on Go Go but my mother moved down to Christmas Creek when I was still young enough to be carried in a coolamon. When they first built that homestead at Christmas Creek they didn't have a bore. So they used to make my mother, and about 10 or 12 other women, collect the water. See those four gallon drums sitting under the table? They used to put a handle in them and they'd make a yoke, like the Chinamen used to use, so those women would be able to carry two of those tins. (Four gallons imperial measurement: about 20 litres - Ed.) Those women would have to walk from the homestead to the waterhole to cart water for the tanks. They would have to do that all day, until about five o'clock in the afternoon.

I remember because I was running after my mother all the way. It's about a mile from the homestead to that waterhole in the creek. They had to fill up the shower-room tanks, fill up the kitchen tanks, and fill up whatever other tanks there were. That was the women's job. They'd trudge up and down from the homestead to the creek. Boy, I tell you those days were really hard. That water was just for the kartiya. They used to work Aborigines hard; they really made them work for their tucker, for their bread and beef.

Early 20th C., wood and water collection.

They used to collect rain water in those days too, you know. When the rain fell on the roof it would run straight into the tank. That was good. But when the water was low those Aboriginal women had to get the water. Year in, year out. They'd trudge down to the waterhole and back with the water. Everyday, all day, except when some rain had fallen and filled the tanks.

That's Christmas Creek that I'm talking about, but I think that it must have been the same for the other stations, even if they could get water from a well. All the stations had a well near their water tank. There was one at Christmas Creek as well, and those women would bucket water up from that too.

But today, if you told someone to get a bucket of water, they wouldn't do it. They'd reckon that it was too hard. See all these rails I've got laying here? I went out about a week ago with an axe and cut them. I've been trying to get this young fella of mine to help but he says, "It's too hard, you should get a chainsaw." You can still see the axe marks on this roof support, though I've sawn the ends off neatly with a hand saw. You see all those posts there? I cut them with an axe too. It's still too early to put them in so I've got them stored here. I reckon that the axe is a good tool, but you try to get one or two young fellas today to use one. They'd stand there and say, "It's too hard! I can't use an axe. Besides, I've still got a carton of beer to drink." They know how to lift up a tin of beer all right.

Boxer Yungar.

I used to be a drinker myself. After Aborigines were given citizenship rights, we used to go in to the Fitzroy Crossing pub and tell Dick Fellon that we wanted rum or whiskey or whatever. He'd say, "Yeah, come into the store." He'd give us as many bottles as we wanted. He had to make his money I suppose, and he must have made a lot of money out of us. I used to drink all that stuff back then, but I began to realize what it does to you. That's when I stopped drinking. Nobody would be camping here with me if I was still drinking; they would have all moved their camps away into the bush.

When our people start drinking they go silly. That's the way I look at it nowadays, good people going to waste. They don't even know why they're drinking. They don't drink the proper way, like the kartiya do in the bar. I've seen it plenty of times with my own eyes. When they grab a carton of beer and walk over to a tree, they're just like a mob of hungry people. They'll grab two or three cans and put them in their pockets. They don't drink slowly like a whiteman; they open up the can and drink it down really fast. Gulp it down like you would with water. Then they start on the next can. That's the way this mob drink beer. You know, the quicker they drink it the quicker they get drunk. That's what they're after - getting drunk.

The Crossing Inn, 1986.

If they run out of beer, they go over to where another mob is sitting. That other mob might be under another tree with a flagon of wine or a bottle of rum or whiskey. This fella who's finished his beer would go over to that other mob and grab their bottle. Now, when he mixes the beer that he's already drunk with that hard stuff, he goes even more silly.

When they drink that heavily, they don't call that one "sister" or this one "cousin," they forget about their skin line. Skin relationships are finished with that mob. Anyone there with a dress on is thought of like a wife. Whiskey takes over all the skin relations. They might grab the first girl they see. "You'll do," they'd say, "Let's you and me go and have a drink, and then we'll go somewhere else." You know, that sort of thing. I remember one girl in the pub told me, "We don't call them jaja or japi or anything now. We call all those who are here husband and wife, we're all mixed now. We don't follow those skin rules anymore." (Skin is the term for a social classification that traditionally determined suitability for marriage - Ed.)

They wouldn't have done that in the old days, no way in the world! The old fellas kept an eye on you. If you did that sort of thing, you'd be finished that night. You'd be dead. That's in the old fellas' time. They'd be watching these young people properly, and they'd keep such things straight and proper according to the old law.

When I was a police aide I was really heavy on the drunks, and I was trying to stop all that carry on. But I couldn't; the grog was too strong. It was leading them away. We're trying to get that skin relation law back clean, but we can't. The grog is too strong. We haven't been able to do anything, right up until today.

In the old days, if you mucked around with a white woman or if a whiteman openly mucked around with a black woman, the police would go in and stop it. I still remember that. But today, a blackfella can go with a white woman and a whiteman can go with an Aboriginal woman, and they can just live together. There's nothing to stop them doing that now. Half the whitemen are getting good now too. They'll live with an Aboriginal girl and if a baby is born, they'll still claim it as their kid.

Noonkanbah wool, 1920s.

Like this English fella I've got living here with my daughter Kate. He still claims his kids. He admitted that he was their father in the courtroom, just the day before yesterday. The magistrate asked him who the father of this kid was, and he said, "Me." Well, that's good. I was waiting to see what he would say. If he had said, "I'm bringing her up but she isn't mine," I would have gone off at him there and then. Now everybody knows that he's the father of this little girl here, and that's good.

This other kartiya here, Mick Monday, is married to my daughter Sandra. He knows how to cook kakaji, or goanna, because I taught him. If we go out for a picnic down by the river and kill goanna, he'll clean it out and cook it for us in the ashes. Well, I reckon if they want to live with us they've got to learn all that.

I like having these kartiyas here, helping me. But some kartiya don't suit me and I get rid of them quick. I wouldn't have a bossy bloke here. He wouldn't last with me for more than a day. Let's say I go to Perth and I want to live with the white people. I'd want to learn their way of living; I'd have to live according to their way. I couldn't live there my way, or they might not want me in their house. See? Well, it's just the same for the kartiyas who want to live here in my camp. They've got to live according to my way.

On Mt Barnett now.

Desmond Bedford, Mt Barnett.

Not like nowadays

The way they muster cattle nowadays is very different, and I've seen enough cattle killed up at Black Hill Yard to know I don't like it. I went fishing up there after the first helicopter came to Go Go. I was wondering what the big heap was over near the yard, so I pulled up to have a look. One of my boys said, "That's the cattle from the helicopter, dad, that's what the helicopter does." "Oh no! No!" I said. I just switched the engine of my Toyota off and put my head down. "No, don't say that!"

Three hundred cattle had been killed and were just piled into a heap. Now, that didn't happen in my time. I might kill one wild bull or one wild cow, a galloping cow. You know, one that always keeps galloping away and you have to keep knocking it back. We used to kill them sometimes for meat; when we were short of a killer we used to kill that bad cow or bull. We'd get rid of it so that it didn't spoil the rest of the mob. But that was all; there were only one or two killed in my time.

This thing that is happening now, good bullocks getting killed, is really bad. I'm just saying what I've seen happen with the helicopter and aeroplane. Us old timers don't like them - me, old Joe Wampi, a few other old fellas here, and a few more who have died since they first came, we don't like seeing those helicopters. Go Go wasn't like that in my time. You'd only have to go two miles from here if you wanted to start mustering in the morning. In just one lap you'd get a thousand head. That's when Go Go had real cattle people. I don't know how many cattle they've got on the property today, but it's almost nothing compared to the old days.

I'll tell you the reason why helicopters kill so many cattle. Now, helicopters don't walk like horses, eh? They're up in the air; the cattle are down here and the helicopter is up there. The helicopter comes and gets in behind the cattle. Say that they want to move them this way, then the helicopter gets over that side. You might as well say that the helicopters gallop the cattle in. Now, for a start, it's no good for the fat cattle. You can only gallop fat cattle for about half a mile and they try to lie down. They get under some scrub, under a tree, or under an antbed. They start to lie down when they can't gallop any more. They get weary in the legs and even the helicopter can't shift them. They get too hot and exhausted, and they die. It kills those fat cattle.

Also, it's not very good for the cattle that survive. When they finally get into the yard they're exhausted and overheated. A lot die inside the yard, and some of the cows abort their calves. The people who buy those animals aren't getting very good meat either, because it's so badly bruised. Not like when they were mustered by horse; it used to be good meat then. There were never any complaints about the quality of the meat in those days. But the helicopter really has spoilt things.

I was in the police force and based at Fitzroy Crossing when the first helicopters came to Go Go. But my boy, young Jimmy, was still working on the station and he used to tell me what was going on. "Oh, we've got a helicopter coming tomorrow," he said one day. I asked where it was coming from. "From the Halls Creek side," he told me, "They're bringing two helicopters over." "What for?" I asked. "Oh, for mustering cattle," he told me. Well, I looked down and scratched my head and said, "Helicopters mustering the cattle; I'd like to see that! But I can't race out there today because I'm busy with police work."

Mt Barnett muster, 1988.

Out of all the stockmen that used to work under me, there were some that were still riding horses, and they used to tell me stories too. Old Killer Pindan told me about the time they took him out near Douglas in a helicopter, and set him down behind the herd. All they gave him was a billycan of water! Ha ha ha! And they told him to bring the cattle back to Sam Maggil Yard. (San Miguel Yard - Ed.) I asked him what happened then?

"Oh no!" Pindan said. "The bullocks and calves were dropping dead all the way back." "How come," I asked, "was it because of the helicopter?" "Too much no good!" he said. "Those helicopters are no good, buddy." Before I went into the police force I had Killer Pindan and all the Killer family working for me. They're good stockmen. "Well, I'd like to find out a bit more from you," I told him, "I want to hear what they did with you." "Kartiya dropped me behind the cattle wanting me to come up on them like a bulldog," he said. "But what were you supposed to do?" I asked, "Where was your horse?"

"No horse!" he said. "They brought me up in the helicopter with only a billycan of water." "You should have gone down to the river," I told him, "had a walkabout and camped there."

I've already mentioned what I saw up at Louisa Yard, you know, Black Hill. What I saw with my own eyes. I asked my boy, "Why are all these bullocks here in a heap?" He said, "That's from the helicopter, daddy. They bring the cattle in around dinner time or in the morning, and they yard them straight away. Those cattle are the ones that dropped dead during the night. They get a tractor to come and pull them out of the yard the next day." That's the time I put my head down. I felt really sad about that. There was nothing like that in my time! One yard I saw had a wing about a mile long, covered in hessian bags. That was for the helicopter, so it can race the cattle in.

Now, those old managers that used to be here, Ted and Arthur Millard, Vic Jones and George Dean, wouldn't have stood for this helicopter business. If they were here today, and saw what the helicopter had done, they would have given the helicopter the boot that day. They would have just told the pilot to take the thing away. Boy! They wouldn't even use a plane for mustering, those old managers, no way in the world! Tim Emanuel used to have a plane, but he would never use it for mustering. He'd just use it to travel round the properties to check how the work was going, or go into Halls Creek or somewhere else. I reckon those old managers had the same sort of feeling for animals as the Aboriginal people have got.

I'm telling you now, if any animal started tonguing, old Ted Millard would come and tell me, "Hey, pull up! There are a couple of cows tonguing there. Pull up for a while." Those old managers were real cattlemen. They would teach us properly if there was something that we wanted to learn. They were men who'd give you a job to do and then leave you alone; they weren't interfering all the time. We had no government looking out for us, and we never got paid, but those old managers were good bosses. Though it's true that they were really only interested in their bullocks.

But today, with this mob, tonguing cattle mean nothing. They'd say, "Look, the helicopter is coming. Good! Look at him chasing those bullocks." They reckon it's fun. Supposing the manager came down to me and said, "You go on a mustering job, and I'll send two helicopters." Well I'd tell him, "No, I won't do it! You get rid of the helicopters and then I'll do the mustering."

They shouldn't clean them out

One thing I want to mention. I'm really sad about what's happening to all the country around here. In the old days there was a lot of bush tucker around, and everything seemed to be alive. But nowadays, it looks as if most of those things have been cleaned out. I haven't seen any emus around for a long while. There used to be a lot of emus around in Ted Millard's time; groups of 5, 10, even 20! Now you go and have a look around and see if you can find any emus. You wouldn't find any. The problem is that they were shot out as soon as the Aborigines got guns in this country. You see, it's mainly the young fellas killing them. They don't listen to the old men any more, so there's no-one to control them, no-one to stop them from shooting so many.

83

Turkey, 1986.

The bush turkey is getting wiped out now; we're getting really short of them. You used to see bush turkey feeding all around here. Back then, if you saw five turkeys over there you might say, "Let's try to get a turkey today, let's creep around that bush and try to get one with a boomerang." You'd throw the boomerang and you'd miss most of the time. Now they brought in that gun, and people go out shooting in a motorcar. "There's a turkey! Bang! Got him!" Well, that man might get 10 turkeys, and he would be taking the breeders too. He wouldn't just kill one or two for dinner, he'd kill the lot. I know that kartiya have been shooting a lot of turkeys too.

In the old days kangaroos were our main food source. The river kangaroos were like sheep right along the Fitzroy River. You know how you see thousands and thousands of sheep in a paddock? That's how many kangaroos there were. Nowadays you won't see many kangaroos at all along the Fitzroy River. What do you think happened? I'll tell you. The kartiya have been poisoning them! I've seen where they've been poisoning them along the river, and around that Seventeen Mile dam, on Calwynyardah and Ellendale stations. Other stations as well. They've cleaned them out. All the kangaroos! They shouldn't do that sort of thing. They shouldn't clean them out!

Kimberley station chopper muster, Napier Downs.

The station managers reckon that the kangaroos ruin the grass or something. You know how the kangaroo eats? You can see where a mob of kangaroos have been eating, because they dig for the roots. They get the sweet stuff at the bottom, they don't go for the top. That's why the managers don't want them in this country. They reckon that they're ruining the grass that should be for the cattle. That's why they say they had to get rid of them. But Aboriginal people will tell you that kangaroos are good for the country. When they dig those holes to feed on the roots, they are helping the grass to grow because they bury the grass seeds.

We used to have big mobs of goats here on Go Go too, well over a thousand. But Tim Emanuel shot the lot. He reckons that goats are no good for this country, because they eat the grass for the cattle. He used to go around every day and shoot all the goats he saw. That was before the Government took over the station.

Now some kartiyas in town here tell me that they're planning to poison the birds. I don't know what type; all sorts I think. You know birds? You can hear them singing in the trees over there. I heard that they want to get rid of them. I don't know what for. Killing birds! What are the birds doing to them? They don't go pulling up the grass and throwing it away. If they're going to start killing the birds off, then the country won't be the same anymore. All the nature will be gone. The country will be dead! Emanuel used to say that it would end up like that. I don't want to see that happen.

This is my mother's country, and my father's and uncle's country. See those black hills over there? That long one runs right up to the Pinnacles. All the caves in there provided shelter for my people in the old times. When the rainy season came they would live in those caves. They used to camp in them, and make a fireplace there during the rainy weather. There are paintings in those caves too, which you can still see in some places. Kartiya might say, "How the hell did they live in there? What was wrong with them?" But that was their house. That was their big town all the way up to the Pinnacles.

The kartiya would get a house built to keep themselves dry, but those Aborigines would go up to the hills. They knew when big rainstorms were coming and they'd move up to the hills. When the rain finished, they'd come out into the open and camp on the plains. During my time people used to run away from the stations and live in those caves. I even camped up there with my mother and stepfather.

I'm trying to get an excision on this place, a little bit of this area that the kartiya call Eight Mile. In our language this place is called Jawarri Ngarri. I want to build up a place here for my children and grandchildren. Rita and I have got nine children - six girls and three boys - and we've got 25 grandchildren so far. Before long there will probably be a big mob of us. That's why I'm trying to think ahead, and that's why I want to get an excision here. So that all those kids will have a home. It doesn't matter if they go to Broome or Halls Creek for a holiday, as long as they've got somewhere to come back to. People have got to have a home for their kids, I reckon.

I don't know what's happening with all this station break-up business. But when I heard people saying that the Government was going to give some of this land back to the Aboriginal people, I had to jump in and try to get this place. I like it here, and it's not in the way of the cattle. You can see that the cattle have got their pad over there near the fence. They don't come over here. I wouldn't have asked for this place if it was going to interfere with the cattle. So I'll just have to wait and see if the Government will give me this little block here. I want to be able to leave something for my family.

Editor's note: The excision of land was made shortly after the publication of *Raparapa*. Jock Shandley and family now live there and around them is a thriving model community, with a further five houses planned for 1993. Its name, celebrated in a spectacular welded gate, is Joy Springs.

helle Brown, unknown girl, Maitland Brown, Clifton Williams, Fitzroy Crossing Kindergarten, 1986.

Phillip Krowan, Fred Russ, Reggie Tataya, Colin Russ, Alfy White, Jock Nowangie, Bruce Pingelliny, Barney Yu Ngarangari.

Rugby Yard, Leopold Downs station.

CHAPTER 3

They can't break us down

Jimmy Bird

Bunuba man (1901? -)

Nyinykuli (Bush name)   Jawanti (Skin name)

My father was a Bunuba man, but a whitefella by the name of Ernie Bird reared me up. I was born on Brooking Springs station, which is near Fitzroy Crossing, but I actually grew up in Derby. You see, when I was still a young boy, Ernie Bird brought me into Derby on a sulky. In those days there were no houses in Derby, and no Woolworths either. The only shop was McGovern's store, which used to be where Woolworths is now. When I was old enough, that kartiya put me to work on Meda station. I couldn't tell you what year that was, but it was a long time ago. I've done a lot of work in my time; I've worked as a musterer, a ringer, a drover and a horse-breaker.

Early days on a Kimberley station.

But I first saw bullocks and horses while I was a little boy on Brooking Springs station. I can remember watching the drovers go by with mobs of cattle, on their way to Derby. There were cattle right through this country, even back then. Kartiya brought cattle into this country when my father was a boy; and they started Brooking Springs up before I was born. It already had a house for the manager, a store, a kitchen, a saddle room, and a cart and wagon shed when I was a little boy.

They shifted that Brooking Springs homestead three times before they got it where it is today. They called it Brooking Springs because it used to be up in Brooking Gorge, on the creek that comes off Fairfield station.

That's where the main place used to be. Before that they had it up alongside the Oscar Range, near where the turnoff is today. There's a spring near there you know. That's where the actual Brooking Springs started from.

I drove cattle for a long time. When I was a young man I drove cattle to Derby from Mt House and Glenroy stations. Mt House only had a humpy, there was no homestead there back then. That was in the early days. It was a long trip. We had to shoe all the horses we used along the road, because it's stony country up there. There were just too many stones.

It wasn't an easy job in my time. You had to look after your horse in the proper way, and work your horse in the proper way. You couldn't knock them about too much. If you worked them roughly they might fall down and break their leg. You can kill them like that. You have to give them a spell too, you've got to let them live quiet for a while. But we had to go from camp to camp like crazy, from camp to camp to camp!

We always used to have an old bullock as the leader for the mob. Old bullocks know everything. Those old bullocks would always pick up our trail and follow along behind. They always kept with the horses and the men, and the other bullocks would always follow their leader. When we started off, those old leader bullocks would notice that we'd started travelling, and they'd get up and follow along behind. We'd walk them until about ten or eleven o'clock, until they started to slow down and look around for tucker. We'd stop them near a waterhole, so they could have a drink, and then we'd set up our dinner camp. The bullocks would camp nearby.

When we started getting ready to move on, that leader bullock would get up, drink some more water, and start feeding about. We would send one man up ahead with the spare horses, the pack horse and all the gear. Then we'd move all the cattle up onto the road. We'd block them, and then we'd go on and pull up a good distance away.

Open range pasture in the 1920s.

Kimberley Pastoral Stations

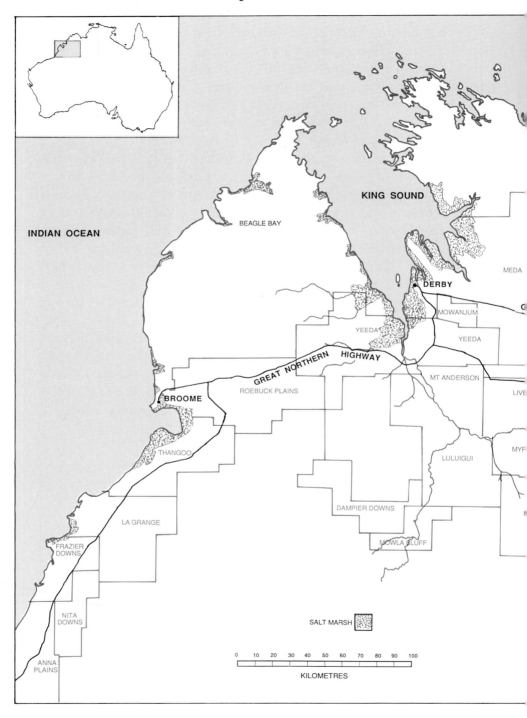

INDIAN OCEAN

KING SOUND

BEAGLE BAY

MEDA

DERBY

MOWANJUM

YEEDA

YEEDA

GREAT NORTHERN HIGHWAY

MT ANDERSON

ROEBUCK PLAINS

LIVE

BROOME

LULUIGUI

MYF

THANGOO

DAMPIER DOWNS

LA GRANGE

MOWLA BLUFF

FRAZIER DOWNS

NITA DOWNS

SALT MARSH

ANNA PLAINS

0 10 20 30 40 50 60 70 80 90 100

KILOMETRES

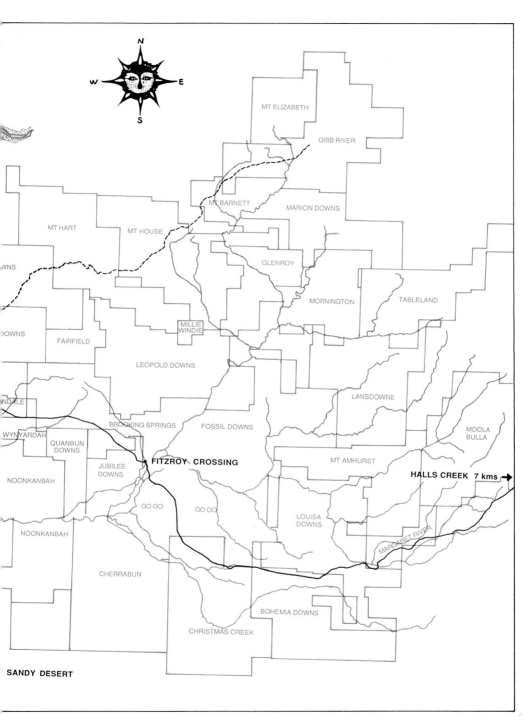

MT ELIZABETH

GIBB RIVER

MT BARNETT

MARION DOWNS

MT HART

MT HOUSE

GLENROY

MORNINGTON

TABLELAND

WNS

MILLIE
WINDIE

DOWNS

FAIRFIELD

LEOPOLD DOWNS

LANSDOWNE

NDALE

BROOKING SPRINGS

FOSSIL DOWNS

MOOLA
BULLA

WYNYARDAH

QUANBUN
DOWNS

FITZROY CROSSING

JUBILEE
DOWNS

MT AMHURST

HALLS CREEK 7 kms

NOONKANBAH

GO GO

GO GO

LOUISA
DOWNS

NOONKANBAH

MARGARET RIVER

CHERRABUN

BOHEMIA DOWNS

CHRISTMAS CREEK

SANDY DESERT

That leader bullock would follow our tracks and come up behind us, and the other cattle would follow him. That's how we'd move them from camp to camp. We used to work a long day. We tailed those cattle all day and watched them, took them down to the watching camp and settled them. Some blokes would be ready with their night horses, and as soon as we got the cattle camped the first fellas would come out to start their watch. We would go over to the camp and take our saddles off. We'd get our supper and go and lie down. By then the first watch would have started work, watching the cattle and singing away. They always used to sing in the early days.

When we were droving from Mt House to Derby, we took the cattle down through Bludger Creek, on to Humber Yard, through Windjana Gorge and down to Oxstone, then on to Kimberley Downs, Boulton, and from there to Milala near the boundary with Meda. We'd ride on past Meda station and make our camp down near Claypan, then head for Native Well, and on to Yabbagoody. Yabbagoody was the last stop before Myalls' Bore, from where we'd take them on to the jetty at Derby. Then we'd be finished.

Derby jetty, early 20th C. steamer on the bottom at low tide.

When we got to Derby, we'd hand the delivery note over to the boss man for the jetty. In those days that was Mr Munga or Ray Russ. They used to come out to One Mile Point to meet us, and they'd cut out what they wanted out there. It might be horny bullocks or it might be nobby bullocks; it depended on what they wanted to ship first. Nobby bullocks are a special breed that don't develop horns. If they were all jammed onto the same boat together, the others might horn them, or that's what the agents were frightened of, so they used to ship the nobby ones first and the horny ones later.

That was how they usually did it. We used to hand the bullocks over to Ray Russ and Munga's people at One Mile, but we still had to take those bullocks right through to the jetty. They used to count how many hundred head they had as they were putting them on the boat. You know, they used to count them properly. We used to put them in the yard alongside the boat, and the workers from the boat would work through the night loading them.

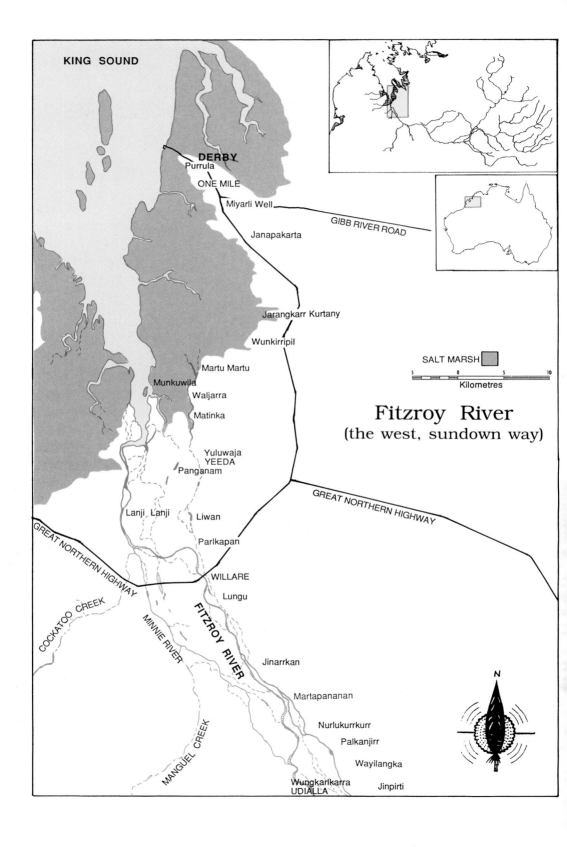

KING SOUND

DERBY
Purrula
ONE MILE
Miyarli Well
GIBB RIVER ROAD
Janapakarta

Jarangkarr Kurtany
Wunkirripil

SALT MARSH

5   0   5   10
Kilometres

Martu Martu
Munkuwila
Waljarra
Matinka
Yuluwaja
YEEDA
Panganam

Fitzroy River
(the west, sundown way)

Lanji Lanji   Liwan

Parlkapan

GREAT NORTHERN HIGHWAY

GREAT NORTHERN HIGHWAY

WILLARE

Lungu

COCKATOO CREEK

MINNIE RIVER

FITZROY RIVER

Jinarrkan

Martapananan

Nurlukurrkurr

Palkanjirr

Wayilangka

MANGUEL CREEK

Wungkarlkarra
UDIALLA   Jinpirti

N

We had a whitefella drover with us in those days, but he never did much. The blackfellas would have to cart all the wood for the camp on their shoulders. They used to cart all the water and do all the other jobs, but the whitefella used to just lay down and read his book. That's all. Those whitefellas would let the blackfellas do everything; all the work around the camp, even looking after their horses.

They'd always have a blackfella along who knew the country, and the whitefella would just bludge on that blackfella. That blackfella would show them where the water was, where to make camp, and how far to go from one camp to the next. It was always that way. The whitefella would take a blackfella along. That's true! In the early days, they used to listen to the blackfellas. But after that, they started putting the blackfella down.

Dam construction on Moola Bulla with Aboriginal labour, early 20th C.

Jimbo Johnson, Mt Barnett.

I don't think kartiya should change the names

Back in those days, if anything went wrong, some blackfella would get a hiding from the boss. A lot of fellas got a hiding. But some were good boys like me. I never got a hiding because I looked at the job in the proper way. I got into a few rows all right, but I didn't get a hiding. A mate of mine, old Snowy Nelson, used to always get a hiding. He's passed away now. A lot of the old people have passed away. I'm the proper head man now.

In those early days, we worked for some rotten men. You know, real rough whitefellas. Not like this lot nowadays; they're working for good fella kartiyas. But I was working for some rough men, whitefellas who would pull their gun out and kill any Aborigines who stood up to them. And there was none of this taking your time to pull your boots on either. No fear! They would use the whip on you. Jimmy Wright, Ernie Bird, Bert Kewen and all those rough white people who were around in the early days treated the blackfellas like slaves.

Those whitefellas used to shoot Aboriginal men and take their women. It happened like this: the whiteman would take an Aboriginal woman, so that woman's husband would grab her in the night and run away from the station with her. Then that whiteman would go after them. If he found them, he'd shoot that blackfella out there and bring that Aboriginal woman back for himself. That's what the whitefellas used to do in the early days. They were real mongrels.

98

Ernie Bird was the worst of the lot. He shot my cousin-brother. That happened when I was about 20 years old. My cousin, Gunna Bird, would have been about 21. He was from Fossil Downs country, a good horseman and good cattleman. One day Ernie Bird started a fight with him. But he couldn't manage him, Gunna was too good for him. After the fight, Gunna went bush, he ran away. We didn't see him until two years later, and that's when he was shot. I'll tell you about it.

In those days Ernie Bird had the mail contract between Derby and Fitzroy Crossing. He and a kartiya by the name of Harry Henty used to run the mail coach, which was a four wheel buggy pulled by a team of horses. It was Harry Henty who caught Gunna and brought him back to the camp. We were camped between Liveringa and Noonkanbah at the time. Straight away Ernie Bird and Harry Henty took him down to the creek, tied him to a tree and shot him. I saw them tie him up but I didn't see them shoot him. Harry Henty had a young Aboriginal fella with him who saw it happen, and he told everyone.

Bert Kewen was almost as bad. They were mongrels, Ernie Bird, Bert Kewen, Billy King, Bill Skinner, Fred Potts, Jimmy Wright and their kind of early days whitefellas. They were all like that. They used the bullet on my people.

Not like the whitefellas here now. Good people came up here later. But there were bad kartiya back in those times. That's true! That was the thing we didn't like. That's why some blokes ran away all the time. Why else would they run away? But those whitefellas would go after them. They'd kill any of our mob that ran away, if they found them. The next time they saw them, they would get out their gun.

They used to shoot them, and then just chuck them in the water. They didn't worry about burying them. No fear! Just chuck them in the water. That's what those whitefellas did in the early days. They were real dirty! Afterwards we came into good people, good whitemen. All the bad people had gone by then, or had died.

In those days, the Native Affairs people were all like policemen. The Native Affairs blokes, the policemen, and the station managers were all mates. If an Aborigine did anything wrong they used to tie him up to a tree, and when sundown came they would come back and give him a hiding. You know, really belt him. If that Aboriginal bloke took his hiding quietly he was all right, they would let him go. But if he fought back, and he was too good for them, they used to shoot him. Not just the manager would do that either; if he fought back with any kartiya, they used to get out the gun. That's true, they'd shoot him. That was still happening back in the 1930s too. They were hard times for the Aboriginal people.

Law ceremony, early 20th C., Kimberley.

Alec Unengen with rope, Johnny Malay, Patrick Echo, Wesley Kuldi.

They used to make us work in the wet season too; we had to make hobbles and rope out of bullock hides. We used to get green hide and sprinkle it with salt. Then we'd come back after two or three days and cut it into strips and make ropes, hobble straps or that kind of thing. (Hobbles are leather restraints attached to the lower leg for limiting the free range of horses left to graze - Ed.)

It's true they used to let us go bush for law business; they let us take the young people out for initiation. But we had to have all the station work finished first. We couldn't just go off when we were ready. We had to wait until the manager said we could go. We usually had Christmas at the station, and after that the manager used to let us go bush until it was time to start work again. But because I was the main horse-breaker I had to come back before everyone else, so I could get the horses ready. I was always the first one to come back. The main bloke who fixed the ropes and things like that had to come back too. It didn't matter so much about the young people, just as long as they came back before the job started to move.

I was a real good horse-breaker. I knew how to handle horses in the proper way, and how to break in horses the proper way. I used

101

to go down and get horses from Anna Plains, bring them back to Meda, and break them all in myself. I broke in a lot of horses down on Anna Plains too. But I didn't get anything out of it. Nothing at all!

Ted Magic (Wumpurul), about to drop onto his bull, Noonkanbah rodeo 1986.

All I got was a buggered-up arm. I was working on Meda when I was thrown off a horse, and broke my elbow. It wasn't all that long ago; I was already an old man. Dave Ledger was the manager there at the time. I guess it was some time in the 'sixties. A lot of people have told me that I should've got some compensation, but in those days there was nothing at all. Nowadays the Aboriginal Legal Service can help people fight for compensation, but in those days there was nothing. There was no welfare in my time, and Native Affairs wouldn't help anybody; they were just like policemen.

A lot of Aboriginal people had accidents with horses and bullocks, but none of them got any compensation. None of them got any money out of it. I don't know what happened to the whitefellas who had accidents, they might have got some money from it. Whitefellas are treated differently, I think. But me and all the other blackfellas got nothing. They didn't give anything to the blackfella; they just robbed us.

When a new manager came along it was the Aboriginal people who taught them the proper way to handle cattle. On Meda it was a native bloke called Meda Frankie that used to teach them. But the Aboriginal people got no money for that either. All we got for our work was a shirt, trousers, boots, hat, tobacco and tucker. We had plenty of tucker, plenty of bullock meat. They looked after us that way. But we didn't get any money. Just tucker, clothes, blankets and a few sticks of tobacco, that's all.

No Aborigine went to the pub to drink in those days, we just stayed on the station and worked all the time. Sometimes we had it good on the stations. There were some managers who were a little bit good and some who were a little bit hard. Lots of different managers.

After we got to Derby with a mob of bullocks and got them into the ship, the kartiya used to buy a few things for us from the shop. Maybe a new shirt or trousers, shaving gear, looking glass, razor, something like that. They used to buy them, and we had to take what they gave us. If you didn't like it, you just got nothing.

In the old days, it didn't matter where we were going, we used to walk there. We'd take a little bit of rubbish blanket and a spear. That's all. It was better, we didn't need a motorcar like today. The woman, man and kids used to walk. I remember a long time ago, maybe even before you were born, I walked from Yeeda station right down through Streeter station to Broome; that's about 200 miles.

I'm a real Nyikina man. Nyikina country extends half way to Fitzroy Crossing. It takes in Noonkanbah, Quanbun and a little bit of Go Go. Some Nyikina people are living there on Go Go, but that's where the boundary with Bunuba runs in. Nyikina country runs the other way right up to Broome. Broome itself is Yawuru country, but it's all Nyikina country right up to there. The Nyikina people and the Yawuru people are all mixed up together nowadays, right through. They share the same law. The Warrwa country comes in on the Meda/Kimberley Downs side; and Bunuba country runs in on the Brooking Springs/Go Go side.

The Nimanburru country runs from Beagle Bay down towards Derby. Beagle Bay itself is Nyul Nyul country. Bardi country comes in at One Arm Point. But all those people have been mixed up together too. This country around Derby used to be a ceremony ground for all those people. It's proper name, it's Nyikina name, is Purrula.

The kartiya are always trying to change the names of places. Like that place they call Native Well. It's called Native Well by white people, but to the Aboriginal people, to the people who used to camp there, it's called Karntimalan. That's the proper name for the place. But if you go past there today you'll find that the kartiya have given it a different name again. I heard that they called it Whiskey Flat now.

Mrs Anne Millard, Mrs Tully, Tom Woodlands (Moola Bulla) at Christmas Creek Station, 1940s. Photo Margaret Wells.

I don't think kartiya should keep changing the names of those places, they should stick to the proper Aboriginal name. They call the old peoples' home in Derby Numbula Nunga, but the proper name for that place is Jiman. I don't know what Numbula Nunga means; it's a Worrorra word.

I was really upset when they changed the name of the Derby Aboriginal Reserve to Karmulingunga, which means "anybody's welcome". They didn't ask me if they could do that, they didn't ask the Nyikina people. Maybe it's part of the kartiya plan to take over the Nyikina country. Or maybe they think all the Nyikina people are dead. But there's plenty of Nyikina people here. There's my family, the Benning family, the Ah Chee family, the Charles family, the Watson family and the Reilly family. They're all Nyikina people and they're still here. Some of these old men were initiated on this ground. I myself was initiated here. So there's plenty of Purrula old men and young fellas here. People who properly belong to this country. They can't break us down; there are too many of us! I've talked to my people about all this, and I reckon they can't take over the Nyikina country. This is blackfella country, this one.

Noonkanbah rodeo.

CHAPTER 4

Not even the cattle

Harry Watson

Nyikina man (1941 -)

Nangan (Bush name)   Jakamarra (Skin name)

I nearly cried

Right up until 1960 I worked on Mt Anderson station, where I was born and bred. I went away for 24 years and then, after the Aboriginal Development Commission bought the lease at the end of 1984, the newly formed Looma/Mt Anderson Pastoral Company appointed me as the manager. That's when I discovered how much the place had changed. When I think back to when we were kids, back to when Canny Rose had the station, I can remember how everything on the station was running well. The house was surrounded by flower gardens and greenery. All the work in the workshop was right up to date. The windmills would never be out of action for more than two days. So there would still be plenty of water in the tanks by the time the windmill was fixed.

It's not like that nowadays. It looked as if everything had been stripped off the place. Not only that, the previous owners had just let the station run right down. When we took over, it was nothing compared to what it was before I left in 1960. I can still picture how this place used to be, I can still see it in my mind's eye.

I nearly cried when I came back and saw how it had been run down. The roof had been blown off the old store and hadn't been replaced. Rubbish had just been left lying around in all the sheds. When I walked into the old shearing shed I found that it had been left in a disgusting mess. There were motors and bits and pieces of iron laying all over the floor, from one end of the building to the other. It took me weeks to clean all the rubbish out from that building, and that was with my brother Ivan helping.

The homestead itself was left in terrible condition too. Now it's starting to fall down, and we don't have the money to do anything about it. But if we let it go any further than it is now it'll cost a lot to repair. I wouldn't like to see it end up like the homestead at Noonkanbah. Anyone who's seen what the Noonkanbah homestead was like 30 years ago will remember that it used to be very pretty. The same was true of Mt Anderson, with it's sparkling swimming pool and beautiful gardens. People who came here back in those days used to say that Liveringa, Mt Anderson, Noonkanbah, and Quanbun looked very grand, even majestic.

Mt Anderson homestead and store, 1916.

Mt Anderson 1988, the same store.

It also saddens me to see the old store like it is. I don't want that building to waste away. I'd like to see a roof put over it, and to keep it as a monument. It dates right back to the beginning of the station, and it served as the store-house for many years. It was the only store we had in those early days. I'd like to see it fixed up like the old people had it. Every year we leave it, the rains wash a bit more of the pindan from between the stones. But it's still a solid structure.

In my mind I can still see the old vegetable garden down by the homestead. It was a beautiful garden too! They used to grow everything in that garden. They didn't have to buy any vegetables at all from the shops in town. Now it's just a mass of Buffel grass. We've tried growing watermelons there recently, but they were just overgrown by grass. (Buffel is an introduced fodder grass now common through parts of northern Australia - Ed.)

The previous owners never equipped nor repaired any of the bores. They just put dams in beside the windmills. The only bores that were working when we took over the station were Number 4 Bore, Bloodwood Bore and the Homestead Bore. There's a windmill on the Homestead Bore but it's in a wind shadow and it only pumps water when the wind is blowing the right way.

As for the fencing? Well I know where all the fences used to be, because I once helped my father do all the fencing work. But when we took over the station there wasn't one fence left standing. They had been pushed over with a bulldozer. And the cattle? There were bugger all; the decent cattle had all been flogged off!

There was supposed to be a bulldozer belonging to the station but that had disappeared by the time we took over. I don't know what happened to the green truck either. That must have been sold off prior to us taking over. They did leave us a few vehicles though. Such as that blue one over there. But that's been a white elephant ever since we put our fingers on it. Cost us a lot of money for nothing. We realised that the head was cracked and decided to send it down to Perth to be X-rayed and welded. But after we'd gone to all the trouble of getting that done, we discovered the gearbox was worn out. As for the station's old grader, we eventually found that on the bank of the dam at Keavie, but it was all burnt out. And it looked to me like it had been deliberately set alight.

The motor that used to sit at the end of the woolshed had been freshly removed, that was clear enough. I think I've seen that same motor at Deep Well on Myroodah station, though I wouldn't know how it got there. When the Aboriginal Development Commission bought this station it was supposed to be a walk-on walk-off sort of deal. But when we told ADC about all the things that were missing they didn't say a thing. To my knowledge they didn't do a thing about it either. There's no doubt that ADC got ripped off when they bought the lease to this property. For the amount of money they spent, a lot of things just weren't here. Not even the cattle!

When I was a kid this station used to support the Rose family, plus two or three dozen blackfellas. There would have been 10 to 20 Aboriginal adults living at Mt Anderson itself, and about five kids (Johnny, me, Victor, Alfie Buckle and Tuckerbox). On top of that my brother Ivan ran another camp at Lower Liveringa. All of us worked, except the really young kids. We'd have to be on the stockwork, in the garden, in the workshop, cooking and cleaning in the big house, or some such thing. Our mother used to work in the kitchen of the big house. Most of the time us kids weren't allowed to play anywhere near the house, but Mrs Rose used to let her son Gayden and me play around the house during the day. She used to take a different attitude to the rest of the Rose family. Though most of the time Gayden and I just played under the verandah.

That was for kartiya

We started getting a lot of jobs to do when we were 8 or 9 years old. They used to give us the job of scrubbing out the swimming pool, which we really enjoyed. They'd also have us greasing hobbles. We used to make hobbles too; we'd even go out and cut wattles to make the pegs for them. Another job was making charcoal for the forge. They sent us down with axes and shovels to where the wattles grew. Firstly we dug a big hole, and then filled it up with all the wood that we cut from the wattle trees. We'd put a fire to it, then cover it over with dirt and the next day we'd go down, dig up all the charcoal and bag it. They would send someone down with a cart to pick it all up when we'd finished.

Vic Taylor, the blacksmith, used that charcoal for his forge. I was his off-sider. He'd get me to work the bellows for him, among other things. Old Vic used to make a lot of things in his forge - hinges, bolts, nuts, and that sort of thing. He also welded pieces of iron by heating them up and hammering them together. He used to do a really perfect job too! I wasn't old enough to learn the trade, though I did pick up quite a lot. I know it's important to get the temperature of the iron just right. If you make it too hot the iron becomes brittle, and if you make it too cold it won't stick together. I didn't learn the skill of doing that, even though I used to watch old Vic do it.

The boss also used to get us kids to work in the garden with him. Not that much of the produce ever made it to our camp. We'd get some once in a blue moon maybe. You know, not all the time. We used to live on corned beef mostly. A bullock would be slaughtered about every fortnight. We'd hang the fresh brisket and other nice cuts in the meat-house, and salt them. That was for kartiya.

Us Aborigines never got to eat brisket in those times. We lived on the less popular cuts and on what we could hunt up for ourselves. There were mobs of kangaroos around then. We'd have no trouble getting enough bush tucker - kangaroos, goannas, and things like that. But all that changed when the kartiya started poisoning them. We looked on the kangaroo as the Aboriginal people's animal, and we knew that it belonged to this country. We didn't like seeing them poisoned. But we had no say on anything the manager did.

Reggie Tataya in meat house doing the beef at Gibb River, 1988. Built 1920s of Cypress logs and corrugated iron.

Fencing seemed to be a never-ending job

When I got a bit older I started helping my father with the fencing. I used to go out in the cart with him. He had two men working with him as well. I'd say it used to take us about three or four weeks to do the frontage fence between Mt Anderson homestead and Lower Liveringa. From there on up to Lungu we'd be fencing along the road as well as the frontage fence. There were three cross-fences too - the boundary fence, another one running up to Turrparn, and one on the other side before Marr. Now and then we'd come across a section where the fence had been washed away. The fences tended to wash away more often out on the open plain.

We'd have to dig the posts back in before renewing the wire. But sometimes a fence would get washed out into the creek and end up a fair way downstream. Then we would have to cut new posts in order to renew the fence. The fencing seemed to be a never-ending job.

When I was a kid, the Government had a policy of sending the police out to grab all the half-caste kids and take them to one of the mission schools. But our boss always knew when the police were going to come out. So he would give the old people a ration and send us off into the bush with them; he'd tell the old people to take us away. When the police party left the station, the boss would send a bloke on a mule to tell us to come back. I'm told that happened several times, though they didn't let us know what was happening. Once we went and stayed at Udialla for a while; but those people were getting shifted out by the Government, so they took us back to the station. Another time they took John and I down into the desert south of Luluigui, down near the top of Geegully Gorge, in Mangala country. We were there about six months or so.

The old people were still scared of the police in those days. Very scared! That was because a lot of Aboriginal people had received hidings from the police. Over the years the police had tied a lot of Aboriginal people up to trees and belted them, and all that sort of thing. So, because the old people were scared of the police everyone else in the camp learnt to be scared too.

Mt Anderson, traditional ceremonial place.

Mt Anderson homestead now.

Moola Bulla station donkey, 1910-18.

Those old people used to talk about what had been done to them and what they had seen done. Aboriginal people knew that they had their own way and had their rights, but the kartiya wouldn't recognise that. White people had control over the Aboriginal. They couldn't spear the kartiya; they had tried that in places but never had any wins. Always kartiya won, and ended up with even more say.

When I was 10 or 12 they started me on the stockwork over at Number 7 Bore. That was when I first rode a horse along behind sheep, and I thought it was really great. In the wet most of the people used to go on holidays, but we stayed on the station along with a few of the old people. We used to love going boundary riding over the wet, checking the fences and things like that. I did that for a few years.

When I got a bit older my main job was horse tailing, which I really loved doing. We had to get up at three o'clock in the morning to round up the horses. We'd have to bring the horses in, hobble them, and fill their nose bags with feed. We'd take it in turns every morning to get the horses. By the time we had fed them and got them ready to go mustering, it would be about four or five o'clock . We used to sit on the fence if we were finished a bit early, and wait for the mustering crew to get themselves ready. The last bloke ready would sing out, and then everybody moved out. There wouldn't be anyone left around the camp; we'd all go off to do the muster.

114

Musterer's plant, Moola Bulla, 1910-18.

They refused to pay me

I left Mt Anderson at the start of 1960. I went into Derby first up, and then went up to Silent Grove and started work with Len Connell. That was up the Gibb River road. I worked with him for 12 months. Old Len was a funny fella, he used to talk to himself! When we pulled up to make our dinner camp, after being on horseback all day, old Len would just take his saddle off and sit down beside it. After a while you'd see his mouth start going, and all of a sudden you'd hear him talking to himself.

In the meantime we would unpack the pack horses, hobble all the horses, collect wood and get a fire going, and put the billy on. When the billy boiled old Len would come along with his quart pot, get his tea and then go and sit against his saddle again. He never used to worry much about tucker. He usually just carried tea and sugar, and a few pieces of corned beef for the road. That was all. Even when he had his swag there, sometimes old Len would be so tired that he'd just lay down beside the fire and go to sleep. He wouldn't even bother unrolling his swag.

It was all cattle work that we were doing: mustering, poddy dodging, and all that sort of thing. (Poddy dodging: calf snatching, before the identifying brand is applied, stealing cattle - Ed.) We'd even go right up into Fish Hole on Mt House property. I was pretty scared at times. People knew that old Len was duffing, but they let him get away with it. I guess I would have been getting about 15 pound a week for doing that.

115

The Fitzroy in flood, 16.3.83, Brooking Channel.

I finished up after a year and headed off for Halls Creek, but I ran into Alfie Buckle in Fitzroy Crossing and ended up working with him. I worked with Alfie for nearly six months. In that time we built two yards for his father Norman Buckle, who was the contractor. But I didn't get a cracker for it. After all the work we did, I finished up with nothing. I couldn't do anything about it so I headed off down river, and I ran into my brother Ivan who was working on the Barrage.

That's the Barrage across the Fitzroy River on Liveringa property; they were still building it at that stage. I was able to get a job there, and continued working there until a crocodile bit me on the wrist. That's why my little finger sticks out like it does; I lost the sinew which works that finger. I can't use it anymore and it's always getting in the road. It's going to get itself chopped off someday! I didn't get any compensation for that. I suppose they thought that it happened in my own hunting time. They ended up sending me to Derby Hospital in the same vehicle as a fella who had been shot dead the same day.

There had been a union dispute between a little fella named David Morrissey and a big bloke named Tom Paul. Tom Paul was one of those tough guys who was always big-noting himself. He always seemed to pick his mark, though he happened to pick the wrong skinny fella on that occasion.

Young David Morrissey used to go hunting with us sometimes. He was actually a half-caste from another race; his mother was a Torres Strait Islander and his father was a captain from an American ship. Apparently he'd had a very good education too. Anyway, Tom Paul finished the dispute by kicking the young fella's guts in. The next thing we knew David Morrissey pulled out a rifle and shot Tom Paul. One shot with a .22 and that was it. He was dead before he touched the ground.

Ivan was standing right behind him, so he was able to catch him and let him down slowly. If it had been a .303 instead of a .22 Ivan might not be alive today. David didn't go berserk with the rifle, he just threw it on the ground and some other fellas led him off to the office. I suppose the police came out and got him. But it was my misfortune to travel back to Derby in the same vehicle as Tom Paul's dead body.

I was laid up in Derby Hospital for four weeks, and by the time I got out the work at the Barrage had just about come to an end. I could have gone to the break-up party but I didn't bother. Instead, I teamed up with a bloke named Mick Driscoll and we went up the range to Oobagooma where we bought some horses from Tom Smith. We rode them down to Wombarella and out to Silent Grove. By then it

117

had started to get too wet for travelling, so we stayed at Silent Grove and did some fencing.

After a while we went down to Millie Windie Gap on Leopold station, and spent three months there building a yard, and living on kangaroos, snakes and goanna. Mick was so mad keen about prospecting that he reminded me of a Donald Duck cartoon. You know the way Scrooge Duck keeps seeing those dollar signs in front of his eyes? One day Mick was looking up at the hill near our camp and he thought he could see where someone had been digging. It was only erosion from the wet season, but he decided that someone had been up there digging for gold. So straight away he was off climbing up the hillside. He asked me to go up with him, but I said, "No thanks, I'll stay here."

While Mick was digging holes up on the hill, I was carting all the timber for the yard. We had to cart all the railings and posts that we cut for the yard on our shoulders. We had no other way to cart them. I had all the timber cut, barked, and piled up ready for Mick to come along, put them in the ground, and put the railings on. But by that stage Mick had decided to chuck the job in and I had to finish it myself. I'll tell you, I had corns on my shoulders from carrying all that bloody timber. But then, after all that effort, they refused to pay me for the job.

So I left Leopold and went over to Tableland where I did some more fencing, before joining up with Karl Madderson and droving a mob of cattle from Tableland to Wyndham. Then I went back to Yeeda and did a bit there, before going over to Jubilee to work stock with the brother for a while. After that it was back to Yeeda for a stint that lasted from 1964 to 1970, then out to Napier Downs under John Wells for nine months. He and I left the station at the same time and I ended up with a job at Derby Hospital. I worked there for 14 months!

Then I thought I'd get on a thing called the RED scheme, which was aimed at keeping people off the dole. (Regional Employment Development, a programme to alleviate unemployment in the mid 1970s, by socially desirable works - Ed.) They gave me a pipe-laying job; we had to renew all the pipes for the Derby water supply. That job finished and I went out to Camballin with the Public Works Department under Jim Robbie. He knew me from the time I was working on the Barrage, so I went to see him and he set me up driving bulldozers. We were making culverts and things like that, doing both the machine work and the concrete. The other day I drove past two of the culverts that I built and I was pleased to see that they were still there.

When I started with the Looma community I was working alongside Vic Green, who was the project officer, under the direction of Sandy Spink, the community chairman. We did all our own pipe laying and put in our own bore without help from the PWD. We did it all through a community work project. We looked after our own generator, all our motorcars and that sort of thing. We had everything running really well. I worked with Vic Green for three years in all. After I worked with him for two years, the community council asked me to assess the quality of his work and they decided to reinstate him for a further year. Then, after Vic left, the community made me the project officer. I was at Looma for a year before the community decided to shift me over to Mt Anderson as the manager.

It took me a while before I found out that my wage had been cut in half. When DAA came along to the community and said, "We'll fix it up so there's money to pay the manager at Mt Anderson as well as the project officer at Looma," we thought, "Good!" But what they didn't tell us was they had taken the one wage and split it in two. They didn't bother consulting the community about it. They didn't mention anything to me, even though I was working for the community and it was my wage being affected. I suppose they thought that an Aboriginal fella was worth only half the wage of a whitefella. I reckon DAA had been itching to cut that wage ever since I took over Vic Green's job. It was only when the brother, as chairman of the Kimberley Land Council, started asking DAA questions that we found out what had been done to our budget. Thankfully, that wage business has been sorted out now and we're looking forward to better days.

Permanent pool on the Fitzroy.

Jimbo Johnson.

CHAPTER 5

He could give it but he couldn't take it

Ivan Watson

Nyikina man (1927 -)

Palpararr (Bush name)   Jampijin (Skin name)

The whip cut right through

I was born on the 22nd October, 1927 at Lower Liveringa station. I only came to know my date of birth through a personal friend of mine, Albert Archer. He was on his way through Lower Liveringa on the day I was born, heading out to a cricket match at Police Camp. He remembered my birth, and that's how I came to know my actual birth date.

Upper Liveringa station, 1930s.

My father had eight children, and he reared us all up on about 30 bob a week. He was an overseer, a head-stockman or whatever it may be called. He used to manage Lower Liveringa, which was an outcamp of Mt Anderson in those days. He always held a high position. He used to look after all the cattle passing through, and the drovers and such used to look after the sheep passing through. When they wanted a hand with the sheep my father used to go and give them a hand with that too. He was actually a bit of a legend along the river in those days. He was a good talker, a good all-round horseman and stockman, and even a good all-round sportsman. A lot of the old fellas used to talk about him, but most of those fellas are gone now.

I can remember very clearly things that happened when I was only three years old. Such as the trips up to Beagle Bay. Father used to take us across-country to see the elder brother and sisters who were going to school at Beagle Bay Mission. That's where they went to school at first. Half-caste and black kids weren't allowed to go to school in Derby in those days. They wouldn't let us! That is until our boss out at Mt Anderson, old Canny Rose, pushed it through. He was a JP and he sent in a letter saying that our father, William Watson, was an important man at Mt Anderson and that it was too far for him to travel with his kids to Beagle Bay. He lost too much time from the job.

So thanks to the efforts of Canning Rose we finished up going to school here in Derby. I started school when I was about 5 years old, but I knew a lot about it from my sisters and older brother. I was supposed to go into lower infants but they put me straight into upper infants. My sisters had already taught me the ABC, the whole alphabet before I even went to school. They had little party tea cups and saucers and we used to go out and play 'housie-housie', that sort of thing. They played at teaching school, pretended to be school teachers. We were keen to learn.

In those days there were only three Aboriginal families sending their kids to the Derby school; that was the Ah Chees, the Buckles, and the Watsons. We were all inter-married too. One of my sisters married an Ah Chee and one married a Buckle. So we classed the rest as our in-laws. After a while people started moving here from Broome, and the next thing we knew everybody started going to school. They made it open to everybody. If it was good enough for one Aboriginal family to go to school in Derby it was good enough for the rest.

But a lot of half-caste children were sent away to missions. I remember them being taken away, even my own age. They were sent all over the country, right down to Perth and the South West. A lot were sent to Beagle Bay, and down to the government-run Moore River Settlement and over to the Forrest River Mission. Others were sent to Moola Bulla, the cattle station also run by the government.

Our two eldest brothers were taken away early in the piece, around 1910 or 1912. That happened years before my time, but our mother told us about it. She thought that they either went to Moore River or to New Norcia Mission down in the south. I think both might have been killed in Gallipoli. They never did come back.

Tommy King, who lives in Broome now, was taken away from Noonkanbah. I know others who were taken away as kids from Myroodah, Noonkanbah and Quanbun. My aunt Lily's son Peter is another one who was taken away. He came back here in '58 or '59 to have a talk with us, but we haven't seen hide nor hair of him since. I hope he hasn't turned into a snob because he owns a farm down near Perth. Apparently he's got a big family down there.

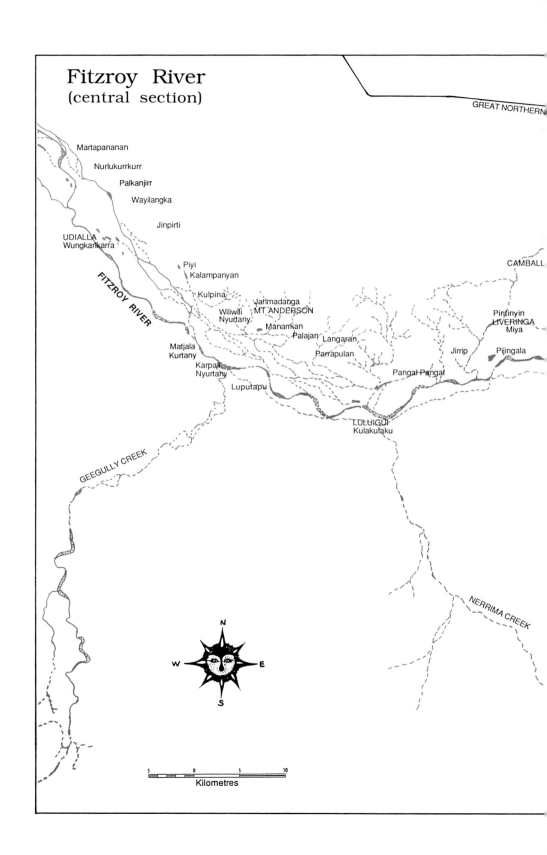

Fitzroy River
(central section)

GREAT NORTHERN

Martapananan

Nurlukurrkurr

Palkanjirr

Wayilangka

Jinpirti

UDIALLA
Wungkarlkarra

CAMBALL

Piyi
Kalampanyan

Kulpina
Jarlmadanga
MT ANDERSON
Wiliwlli
Nyurtany
Manarrkan
Palajan
Langaran
Pintinyin
LIVERINGA
Miya

Matjala
Kurtany
Parrapulan
Jirrip
Pijingala

Karpala
Nyurtany
Luputapu
Pangal-Pangal

LULUIGUI
Kulakulaku

FITZROY RIVER

GEEGULLY CREEK

NERRIMA CREEK

N
W E
S

5   0   5   10
Kilometres

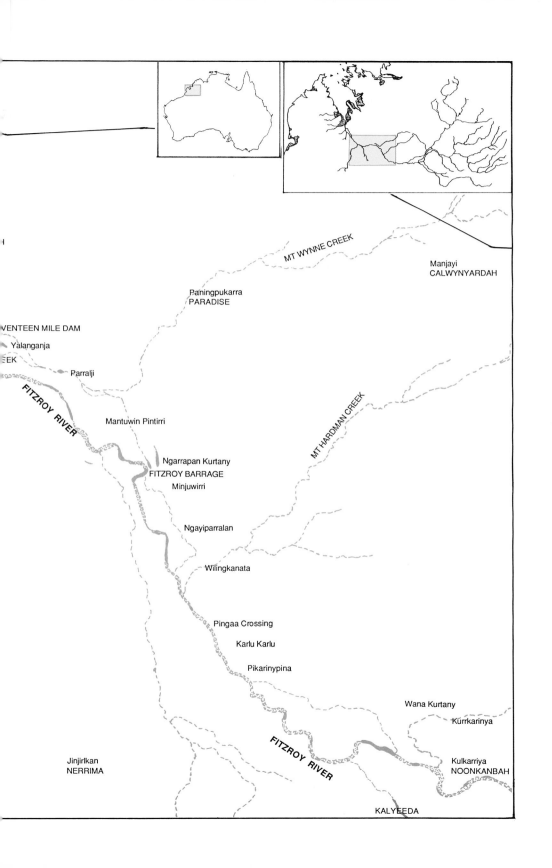

MT WYNNE CREEK

Manjayi
CALWYNYARDAH

Paningpukarra
PARADISE

VENTEEN MILE DAM

Yalanganja

EEK

Parralji

FITZROY RIVER

Mantuwin Pintirri

MT HARDMAN CREEK

Ngarrapan Kurtany
FITZROY BARRAGE
Minjuwirri

Ngayiparralan

Wilingkanata

Pingaa Crossing

Karlu Karlu

Pikarinypina

Wana Kurtany

Kurrkarinya

Jinjirlkan
NERRIMA

FITZROY RIVER

Kulkarriya
NOONKANBAH

KALYEEDA

Moola Bulla station youngsters, 1920s.

There are only the odd ones who have ever come back. I met two girls last time I was in Perth who are still seeking their parents today. They were part-Chinese girls, so I told them they should try looking in the Wyndham area because that's where most of the Chinese were. There were more Chinese up in that area on account of that fella up in Darwin who brought them out, 600 at a time, for his gold mine. And of course they drifted down to the Kimberley. There were quite a few Afghans around too, especially during the time of the gold rush at Halls Creek. There were the odd Japanese around there too.

The white people use the name "half-caste" for some kids, but to us they're all Aboriginal people. The problem is that the fathers of those children didn't say, "That's my kid and I'll leave it with my name." So those kids had to wear whatever name they were given, such as Billy Billycan, or Harry Stirrup, or Joe Leather. Those were the types of names they gave to Aboriginal people. They'd name them after any old article! I feel pretty angry at the way they broke families up and sent those kids away, often never to see their parents again.

I left school when I was 12 because the school teachers couldn't put up with me. So I was sent down to Yeeda and started doing stockwork with a fella called Stumpy Frazer. He was a very hard man. I though my father was hard, but that bloke was even harder. At any rate, it was discipline I needed and discipline is what I got. I could ride a horse when I was 4 years old, so I had no problem riding a horse and doing mustering when I was 12.

Harry Watson on horse. John Watson.

Alec Unengen lighting up for branding with an iron in the fire, Mt Barnett.

Alec Unengen holding a leg, Patrick Echo marking, Olfin branding, Desmond Bedford, Anthony Numendumah.

Jimmy Olfin, Alec Unengen.

I never got any pay during that whole time. I was there 11 months with Stumpy Frazer and in all that time all I would have got was two sets of clothes, a pair of riding boots, a hat, and three feeds a day. That was my pay. But the reason my father sent me there was to get a bit of discipline.

I still carry whip marks on my back today from Stumpy Frazer. I remember one time he whipped me because I had kicked a calf in the ribs. Then another time he whipped me for sticking a Conkerberry bush under his horse's tail. You know if you put something under a horse's tail it'll clamp it's tail down onto it? Well the Conkerberry bush, or Kungkara as we call it, produces good edible fruit but the whole bush is covered with little prickles. When a horse clamps its tail down on to one of those it'll buck like blazes and throw its rider.

He used to do that to us, but we weren't allowed to do it back. He could give it but he couldn't take it. We thought that playing the act back on him would be a bit of a joke, but it wasn't as far as he was concerned. I was wearing a dungaree shirt and the whip cut right through the shirt and into my back. He would have kept at it too, except a group of other fellas there stopped him.

Once that mustering season was over and shipping had all been done, I left Yeeda and went to see my sister who was living on Liveringa, at the Willumbah outstation. I spent a few weeks with her and then I finished up getting a job nearby, at Paradise. I was 13 and I stayed there until I was 17. That's where I got my four years experience with sheep work. I did a bit of everything really, repairing windmills, fencing, horse-breaking and mustering. I did whatever was going, though it was mostly stockwork.

We were actually the second shed to the Liveringa Pastoral Company, so when we needed more hands they would send over some people from Liveringa. In the same way, if they needed a hand at Liveringa we used to go over there from Paradise. We were mainly just looking after the wethers and weaners. All the ewes were scattered around Six Mile and Yalanganyja. That's where the breeding part of the operation was. We used to hold the wethers right up the top near Pyramid on the boundary with Noonkanbah.

We'd do the wethers and the lamb marking. If they're strong enough you can cut lambs when they're as young as one day old. From the time they're cut they're called weaners. Once they've cut their first two teeth they're called hoggets, and when they have four teeth (around 4 years old) they're called wethers.

Upper Liveringa station shearing shed, 1916.

Most of the Aborigines that were working at Paradise in those days are living at Looma now: Banjo, Buddy and Donald are all living there. Dick lives in Derby at the old ration camp. There was a family that had come across from Townsville working there too. That was the Shadforths. That's where I first met them. There was the old fella Harry, his wife, the two sons Henry and Richard, and their little girl. They're all split up nowadays; Henry lives in Derby, Richard lives over at Beagle Bay, and the lass ended up marrying Bill Prowse.

"Hey, you better put that away!"

The Second World War was going on at the time when I was working in Paradise. They had one of those radar stations on the top of the hill at Paradise, and they had a big airforce base at Noonkanbah. There would have been about 600 army and airforce personnel there, as well as the DOI and the people working on the station itself. (Dept. of the Interior - Ed.) You name it, they had it. They had beautiful big airstrips there, built for the Department of the Interior by Bell Brothers and Gascoyne Traders. They had air-raid shelters for all the planes. It was all set up so that the planes could go off onto different tracks and into big shelters. They had Mosquito Bombers there, as well as the Lancaster, the Boomerang, and the Kittyhawk. The Spitfire wasn't out here, but they had everything else.

They had a district platoon up here headed by Sergeant Mason. You can see their inscription on the old concrete swimming pool at Myalls' Bore today. Actually, I remember Sergeant Mason from when the mob used to camp in Derby. The army had all that area from Myalls' Bore right out to where old Mowanjum is. All that area, including the area right back to the bend in the road, was taken up with fuel dumps. They used to use convoys to cart provisions from there out to the base at Noonkanbah.

131

I didn't have much to do with the mob at Noonkanbah except for going to watch the boxing there on weekends. Then one day they put me into the ring to fight a serviceman who must have been all of six foot six. (198 cm.) That was my first fight and I came home with two black eyes. But I never lost a fight after that.

I had a lot more to do with the fellas based at Paradise. They only had a small squad there but they were good blokes. The medical doctor, a young fella by the name of Kennadare, used to go horse riding with me. We were out looking for a killer one day when my horse put its foot down a goanna hole, broke its leg, and came crashing down on top of me. I broke two ribs, one collarbone, and dislocated the other collarbone. Dr Kennadare rode back to Paradise and came to collect me in a four wheel drive vehicle. I was laid up in an army tent at Paradise for three weeks after that. They really treated me like a king too.

Most of us stockmen joined up with the Home Defence. Actually, I was the youngest one in the platoon. They put us all through a three or four week training course at Liveringa with Major Mitchell, Sergeant Mong and Sergeant Buckingham. Old Buck and I became great friends years later when I was the head stockman at Yeeda. We were the last of the Light Horsemen, and we were going to be sent from that platoon into the tank squadron if the need arose. That's where the changeover was. But they didn't send us overseas, not even to New Guinea. They wouldn't take us! I suppose it was because we were the meat suppliers, working on the stations as we were. They wouldn't take any of us from the stations, they must have regarded it as an essential industry. But they took us for training, for so many weeks of the year, just in case they needed us on the Home Defence front.

They made my father a corporal because he knew the country and knew the environment. The managers were a bit jealous about that, because a coloured fella was made a corporal and they were a lower rank. Anyway, after we had done the training we had a mock battle; they put us under fire and all that sort of thing. They put me in the mortar platoon with Len McAlear and another fella, and taught us to operate the mortar-gun. They also taught us how to use the different types of machine gun: the Lewis, the Owen and the Bren. They even put us under fire from them.

Then they put us on the range to see who would score the best in a shooting contest, and had a nomination fee of 10 shillings each. Our boss at Mt Anderson, Canny Rose, won it and my father came second. I was the youngest in the competition and came third. Old Pearson Logue came fourth. All of us came from Mt Anderson. We always used to have a practice shoot at Mt Anderson if we had nothing to do on a Sunday. So, that's how we came to win the shooting contest.

Then our Home Defence platoon had a mock raid on Noonkanbah and we took the whole base. The 40 of us captured the whole lot of them: the army, the airforce and the DOI. They knew that we were coming too, we had told them to expect a mock raid anytime within a three-day period. My father was the leader of that raid. He took us cross-country in a truck at night.

We had a bit of a hitch right at the start as we were going through Paradise. The mob there captured a couple of our men, Henry D'Antoine and another fella. They locked them up and were going on to Noonkanbah to warn them that we were coming. But when they got out to where their motorcars were parked they found that they were gone. Henry and this other fella had freed themselves, got into the only two motorcars they had there, and driven them away. So they couldn't go anywhere. The other fella stopped at Butler's Bore in case there was any emergency, and Henry came on to let us know what had happened. As it finished up, those two fellas captured the whole Paradise radar installation.

The rest of us continued on until we reached Luby's Yard near Mickey's Swamp, where we pulled up to have a baked supper. It would have been about two o'clock in the morning, so we thought we'd put the billy on and have something to eat before we did our raid. While we were looking around for wood I found somebody's swag, still warm, as if the occupant had only just left it. We found out later that it belonged to an old native fella, old Toby's father, Broom Broom. Bill Henwood had posted him there and told him to warn them if he saw anyone coming. But he must have really thought that we were the enemy, so he just took off.

He didn't bother stopping to tell the boss, he just went past the camp at full speed telling all the natives that the Japs were coming, and he kept on going! They didn't see him for years after that. So the boss never got his message. All they got was, "The Japanese are coming!" You see? Well, naturally, those people thought that the Japs were coming. When they were asked who had told them, they said it was old Broom Broom. They ended up telling us the yarn the next day, after we'd captured them all.

Anyway, to get back to the story, after having our supper we headed across to P Hill (Wanpanpuru) and then followed the river. We parked our truck five miles up-river at about three thirty a.m. and then walked the last leg, carrying our blueys. (Blanket roll or swag, named after the standard issue grey-blue woollen blanket – Ed.) We got to Noonkanbah just as day was breaking and that's when we took them, right at daybreak. We sure took the manager of Noonkanbah by surprise. Henwood was out having an early morning wee, and old Kim Rose called out to him, "Hey, you better put that away!"

Then we took over the old cubby there, which I think was the DOI camp. The cook they had there, old Bluey, was a personal friend of ours but she was a very hard woman. She finished up flogging old Tommy D'Antoine out of the kitchen with a pot and pan! She was the only one at Noonkanbah that won a battle. She finished up marrying Jimmy Neighbour and you know, since then I haven't been able to remember her original surname. I think she's living up in Wyndham now. Anyway, it just goes to show that if you know the place where you're operating, you have a much better chance of defeating an opposition that doesn't know those things.

I've heard that there are two Japanese Zeros stowed away in the bush between here and Mitchell Plateau. I read an article in the the paper about a Japanese bloke who came over here trying to locate them. Apparently he's the nephew of the fella that led the raid on Pearl Harbour, and he reckons he visited the coast here during the war. He was just an ordinary sailor on a submarine, or boat of some sort. Apparently they had a little airstrip up there and had two Zeros, which they parked under a big rock shelf. If those Zeros were found they would be worth a lot of money. The Japanese were so close, but the terrain they bumped into was unbelievable. They just couldn't move. All they could do was to get in the plane and fly off. Apparently they pulled their blokes out of that base towards the end of the war, when they were getting cleaned up.

By the time I turned 17 I'd been at Paradise for a while, and so I decided to go back to Mt Anderson. I was there off and on after that. I spent four years there in succession and then I came back for another five. Or something like that. I was running that place for nine months of the year towards the end of the time when the old fella Canny Rose was sick. That was after our father had died. We were on top of all the work, we had all the windmills going and we had everything well organised. We had all the jobs worked out, day for day. The cattle section was being looked after well too. We were able to do things such as keeping a check on the cattle and pulling them out from the bogs in the dry season. Nowadays we're too pushed for time to do those sorts of jobs.

Droving near Fitzroy Crossing, 12 Mile, Mantuwa and Warimpah. Photo Australian Panorama.

We used to take our dinner with us and ride around the pools on a horse. If we saw a beast bogged we'd try to throw a rope over its head. Otherwise we had to walk in and put the rope over its horns. If we couldn't do that and he was too bogged to get it around his leg, we had to put it around his waist, or wherever we could get at. Then we pulled him out with a bronco horse.

We used to set it up so the rope went over our saddle and around underneath. It had a ring on the end, which could be hooked onto the near-side of the saddle with a bronco hook. Nowadays you would just throw a rope over them, put your vehicle in reverse, and pull the beast out.

I left Mt Anderson to take up the head stockman job at Yeeda. When I arrived at Yeeda there was supposed to be this amount of horses, that amount of cattle, and so many bullocks in the bullock paddock. But they weren't there, the floods had wiped them all out. Cattle and horses were hanging from the trees. It was a very sad sight. I reckon that the floods this year (1986) would have resulted in the same situation. So in order to do the Yeeda mustering that year, we had to do what we're doing at Mt Anderson now. We had to break in the horses before we could muster.

As the head stockman at Yeeda, I had my first opportunity at cutting beasts out for sale. When I had worked cattle as a kid with my old man he always did the cutting out and I used to work the face for him. By that I mean I would take the beasts he cut out over to where the other stockmen were holding the beasts we wanted to ship off. The ground between the mixed mob and the cut-out mob is called the face. But then the owner at Yeeda started telling me, "Cut that one out, and that one, and that one." Well, his choices were beyond me. In all the time I watched my father cutting out, I never saw such scrawny little steers being cut out for shipment. So I said to the manager, "If your cutting out is so good, I'll leave you to do it yourself." That's how I left Yeeda.

After that I did a bit of yard building at Logue's, and then I took on truck driving for old Bill Smith. He would drive one truck and I'd drive the other. We had to use flat-tops because we couldn't take semi-trailers on those rough gravel tracks. There have been a lot of changes up here since then. It used to take us a week to get to Mt House from Derby, where nowadays on the bitumen road it only takes four hours. But we had to go the long way round, via Millie Windie Gap, around Rifle Point; then we'd go past Saddler's Spring and carry on up to Mt House. From there, if we went one way, we could take in all the stations to the south-east: Glenroy, Mornington and Tableland. Or going the other way, we'd take in Mt Barnett and Gibb River. Mt Elizabeth wasn't there at the time – that's the station. This all happened around 1948.

Broncoing calves, 1930s.

I'll tell you, Bill Smith was a good boss, even if he wasn't much use with the loading and unloading. When we went on a trip he used to bring everything. He'd have boiled lollies for the station kids, Deadwood Dick books, and his tuckerbox was always full. There was never any shortage of tucker! If we got bogged, he wouldn't try to dig the truck out. No way in the world! There was no way he'd rip and roar it through the bog hole either. He wouldn't risk burning his truck out. He would just camp there until the track dried up; and he would get out the lollies, the Deadwood Dick books, and the tucker. Old Bill and I were tied up together quite a lot through his trucking business. Later on, when I was about 27 years of age and a married man, I took up cabbing here in Derby. But I still used to cart wool from Mt Anderson in old Bill's semi-trailer. That was a better road and the old truck could take it.

The Verandah Boss

Once in the wet I was building a woolshed. They had a Russian, George a'Linsky looking after the place, he was the verandah boss. That's what I call 'em. We've had different ones like old Doug Mew, he used to be an ex-manager over Kulakulaku, but to my eyes he had positions that he shouldn't have held, you know, because nowhere was he as good as that. He might have been pencil-wise, but that's about all that gave him his job, carried him. Ability he had bugger all, he had nothing, lose himself in the twilight that fella.

I said to this Russian, "What about the boss doing a few days work?" We were building the woolshed. So he came out and I gave him a big hammer. I remember, he had three swipes at the standards, and he said, "Well bugger that - who's gonna do this? Nobody!" Put it down and away he went. George a'Linsky his name was, I wonder where they would have got him from?

You know and I know, they're what you call remittance men, who are chucked out of their country, they're paid to stop away - and that's what he was, a remittance man. Fellas from aristocrat families, and there you are, I know quite a few used to be down here in this river country and I found out, asking them personally because I don't hesitate, I ask anybody. All they can do is punch you in the nose, or try to hit out, you know. They'll say, "Oh I'm a remittance man." See the family pays him big money to stop away.

He worked at Double Ringer with Canny Rose's brother Kim, Double Ringer, and I don't know what was the outlook of the boss, why they sent him over there. I didn't like the idea but I never said nothing because that was their business. I thought it was wrong sending a remittance man to look after me. Was he looking after the station, or was he looking after me?

I was left in charge of all the stock, but I had a Russian looking after me! You know, I couldn't work that one out. I was in charge of all the mustering camp, all the stock, I had to get sheep into position for shearing, I knew what I had to do, but why put him looking after me? He didn't poke his nose in though, he didn't go that way with me, he seemed quite pally and he used to eat this yoghurt.

I can't stand it, yoghurt; but he made these yoghurts. We had goats there, and he used to skim the milk off, put it away in the freezer, all the water out of the milk, and when it started to float he'd skim that off. Used to get strawberries - I don't know where he got those from, must have been Perth or somewhere. Strawberries! And yoghurt, that was one of his main meals, strawberries on the yoghurt. And he used to get Players cigarettes, 50 in a tin. Always Players, big tins, that sort of thing. A remittance man, George a'Linsky. In the 1950s, '55 or '56 it was.

I got married in '54. Old Rose, he says to me, "How long you gonna be, gettin' yourself a wife?" So I went into Derby, and came back that afternoon with someone. He said, "Hullo, what you doing?" He was surprised. "That's quick." I had a woman, see. I said, "Trial run, hahaha." And Rose, he said, "Hmm." I think the old bastard wanted to give me a hand.

After that I got a job in Derby with Lou Kent, and got my ticket as a powerhouse engine driver. Lou owned the powerhouse which supplied DC power to Derby. I operated the plant for around 18 months to two years, along with another coloured fella by the name of Elwin Brown. Lou's old powerhouse used to be down near the jetty, just where the DAA offices and the Tourist Bureau are standing now.

Then I spent three years working on the construction of the Seventeen Mile Dam and the Barrage, as a truckie. I was driving big old AEC and Foden trucks for a fella, and I finished up owning his two trucks. He left them to me! So from then on I was my own boss. The company used to pay us for driving as well as paying us by the load, which was all right. That took me into the 'sixties. After that I came back into Derby and used the money I had made to buy land at five shillings an acre. I tried to start a farm called Goodie Goodie just out of town, along the road to the Leprosarium. But everything we tried to grow there came up and went yellow. So we gave that away and shifted to Logues the following year.

Then I took up taxi driving again, this time for old Ian Todd. I finished up owning one of the cabs, but then the black book got too heavy. So I said, "Bugger this!" There must have been over $20,000 owing to me in that black book. I just put it down to experience and gave cabbing away again.

The whole eleven hundred went over the top

I've done a lot of droving too, back in the days when I was still young and single. The first droving trip I did was with sheep; we drove 3,000 head of wethers from Paradise over to the Leprosarium near Derby. Sheep were a lot harder to drove than cattle, because you have to build a break-yard for them every night. We used to leave each yard at four o'clock in the morning and we could only do about eight miles in a day. By the time it was eight o'clock we would have done the stage for the day, and we'd just mill the sheep around so they could have a feed while we built the next yard. We had sheep dogs with us and they'd keep an eye on them as well. We'd only need to build enough of a yard to hold them for the one night, so we made it mostly out of bushes.

In 1947 the elder brother Blue and I lifted the biggest mob of cattle that ever came down the Fitzroy River in one mob. That was 1,100 head, which we had picked up at Brooking Springs and Leopold Downs. Blue was the head drover and I was the acting cook. We started off with just the ordinary plant. We had some old fellas and four other young stockmen with us, one of whom was the horse tailer. Well, we had a picnic!

The cattle rushed almost every night from Broken Wagon on. The only night they didn't rush us was just before Six Mile on the other side of Liveringa. We had a good crew of men with us, but we got to the stage where we were so desperate that Blue had to send Paddy off to get extra men from Leopold, Brooking Springs, and wherever he could get them. We finished up with about 12 or 13 men when we reached Yeeda. They were all Aborigines too, there wasn't a whitefella amongst us.

Nerrima station, Green Springs, 1963. John Watson second from left, Johnny Sheen second from right.

Cattle coming down for shipment, north-west, 1916.

Droving becomes a dangerous game when the cattle rush. When a mob of bullocks take off together, it's just like an explosion coming out of a cannon. There's a big report and they're all gone. They clean away everything in their path too! At Box Flat, near Lower Liveringa, they wiped out our entire camp: swags, blankets, tarps, tucker, billycans. The lot. They flattened our cart too. The whole eleven hundred went over the top of it; you couldn't have picked up a thing from it afterwards. It was drizzling rain that night too, and all we had left was what we had on our backs.

Fortunately all the horses got out of the way; it was a good thing we had some smart night horses with us. So we had to stay camped at Box Flat the following day, and had to get a loan of clothing, blankets and gear from Canny Rose. Of course he knew us. He gave us pack mules, pack bags and provisions so we could continue the journey into Derby.

Fred Russ, Gibb River station owner in 1988.

Whether cattle rush or not depends on how they feel, but it's always a bad one that kicks them off. At first we thought that it might have been wild cats. Then we started looking around for a real outsider, you know, a bad beast. Eventually we worked out that the culprit was a poddy bullock, the milking cow's calf. He must have weighed about 14 hundredweight (700 kg. - Ed.), and he used to lay right alongside the fire. He was so quiet that I used to sit on him! But, I said to big brother, "He's the cause of it." The rest of the mob would be gone and he'd still be there. We realised in the end that he used to stand up in front of the fire and cast his shadow over the mob. That's what was starting them off. So after that we tried to get him to go around and sleep behind the fire. When we got him to Derby, and tried to put him down the cattle race on the jetty, we found out that he wouldn't fit through the last bit going onto the boat. So we slaughtered him in the pound yard and gave him to the town folks as a Christmas present.

They were never part of the country

So that was droving! I only did that for two years with Blue, I wasn't too wrapped up in it. But I'd like to see all that come back, because I've found that there's a terrible loss of meat when cattle are trucked. If you counted over the last twenty-odd years of trucking cattle, you might find as much as 25% of them have been so badly bruised that the meat has to be thrown out. That would be an awful lot of meat going to waste. So I reckon that the only way to get cattle to the meatworks, or wherever they're going, is on the hoof. Do away with the trucks, and get the horses back again!

When I was only a kid of 7 or 8 years old, they started building what they called a wet weather track. The main track ran along the river frontage so, in those days, you had no choice but to follow the

Fitzroy River around. Of course, it's prone to flooding in the wet season. The new road they built was just pindan track. From Nobby's Well to Derby it ran about where the highway is now; following the telephone line. It was built prior to the Second World War by a mob called the West Kimberley Roads Board. Those fellas built that road using picks, shovels and rakes.

In a lot of places that road is still there. There are some sections that we still use today. It's actually a marvellous road for the simple reason that it was all placed by hand. I think they made that road four metres across, just a one vehicle lane. It used to run through all the stations, right through Yeeda, Lower Liveringa, Mt Anderson, Upper Liveringa, Noonkanbah, Jubilee, and on to Fitzroy Crossing. If you drive through those stations today, you'll notice that handmade road. It goes right past what they call Willare today, where the roadhouse and the bridge over the river are. Maitland Buckle was the working foreman on the construction of that road for the West Kimberley Roads Board. (I remember his wife, in later years, was living at Myalls' Bore with her second husband, a fella by the name of Smith.)

From my recollection Maitland Buckle used to have a donkey team, wagon and whatnot before he got that foreman job. I remember all those old teamsters coming in to pick up a load of wool or to bring out supplies and station gear. When they pulled into Lower Liveringa all us kids, all the brothers and sisters and I, used to go down to meet them. They got to know us so well they used to bring us back a four gallon tin of boiled lollies. That's why I got no teeth today; from chewing boiled lollies! Even today I could name just about all the teamsters who used to pull into Lower Liveringa. To this day, I haven't forgotten them.

I would say that they usually had up to 20 donkeys in a team, but sometimes for a particularly heavy load they would use up to 26. It all depended on the load they were carrying.

They would see what their progress was like, and if they needed extra donkeys they would stick them in. They had a bell-bag underneath the wagon with all the extra chains, harness, and collars, and they always had spare donkeys. They always had a mule and a saddle with them too, and an Aboriginal off-sider. It would be his job to round up the donkeys for them. The donkeys were great workers because they knew their positions on the team. The teamster would just give them the order and they would all line up to get their collars and chains put on for the duty of the day.

It hurts me to see how they shoot donkeys out today. They call them vermin; the poor buggers! Those old donkeys actually made the Kimberley, you know? Today they're called vermin. We didn't bring them into this country and they don't actually belong here. They never were part of this country. But we don't regard them as vermin. If certain people had the chance, they would shoot the blackfellas like they're shooting donkeys, because they've got no jobs for them!

Noonkanbah station woolclip, 1919.

Cattle at watering trough.

I was born during the depression years, and I can still remember all the people who came through looking for jobs. I had thought to myself that they must have come up from Port Hedland, but I think some of them came from as far away as Perth. Especially the shearers. That's when the blade-shearing was on. If they wanted work, they just had to walk or get here the best way they could. Some were carrying their blueys, some came with buggies or carts, and there were even a few pushing wheelbarrows with all their gear in. Quite a few lost their lives getting up here too. There are quite a few graves between Broome and here, and between Port Hedland and Broome. I think they had perished from lack of water. It's part of the history of the area.

There were two fellas who came out to Lower Liveringa looking for work. Canny Rose's father old G.C. Rose gave them a job putting down that deep well. They put that down for a shilling a foot, plus three feeds a day. Of course, in those days the main thing was to get three feeds a day. During the depression jobs were few and far between. Still, it must have been hard work. I think that well is 60 feet deep, so those two blokes would have only got three pound for doing that job. But that's all they wanted in those days, as long as they got their three feeds a day they were well off. That's why we used to be a bit better off on the stations, because we got our meat free. We weren't a rich family in money or anything, but we were rich in our own little way. We always provided a feed for anybody who came past there.

If they couldn't get a job along the way, they'd finish up in Halls Creek at the gold diggings. People were always chasing that gold at Halls Creek. They'd spend their days digging around for enough gold to survive on. You would have thought that all the gold around Halls Creek would have been cleaned up during the depression days, but they're finding more gold there now than ever before. They're using modern equipment too. Those fellas in the early days had to work hard, they didn't have bulldozers or the other things which are used today.

Now, I want to tell you a few things about Myalls' Bore, just outside Derby. The proper name for that place is Miyarli Well. But when the kartiya get hold of the name for a place, they don't actually say it the way we do. They started off calling the place Myalls' Well, which you can see was a distorted pronunciation from the proper name. Later on they started calling it Myalls' Bore.

The thing that the tourist brochures call "the longest cattle trough in the southern hemisphere" was built somewhere between 1912 and 1920 by a bloke called Joe Griffin. It was fed by an artesian flowing bore, so the water was warm when it came out of the ground. It used to go to the bore's clackvalve, so that when the trough filled up the clacker would shut it off and divert the excess out through another pipe. That way the bore didn't have to stop running. The excess used to run down to a swamp nearby, which had bullrushes and all those sorts of plants growing there. It used to be nice and green. In fact, it looked much better than it does now. Of course, the original flowing bore has been blocked off now.

But there's another concrete trough in the bush nearby which pre-dates Joe Griffin's one by 10 or 20 years. I first saw it when I was about 17 years old. My father showed it to me when we were droving some bullocks from Mt Anderson to Derby. I call it Myalls' Bore the First. The last time I saw it would have been 34 years ago, when we were droving a mob of sheep which had been shipped from Carnarvon to Derby. We were taking them back to Mt Anderson. That's how long it's been. But I still remember where it was; I remember it was alongside a gum tree.

Harry Watson at the older Myalls' cattle trough.

iyarli Well - Myalls' Bore.

There was a well alongside it too, though that's filled in now. They had to have a well near the middle of the trough and not too far from it, since they had to use a whipping set-up to draw the water from the well. I haven't actually seen the whipping set-up, though I've seen a rough sketch of one. I believe they were also used down the Canning Stock Route. They used to have a donkey, mule or sometimes even a horse hooked up to it. The animal's job would be to draw the water up, but then there had to be a bloke standing there to pick the bucket up and empty it into the trough.

Myalls' Bore, that was the meeting place for the drovers in the early days. After leaving there they would move their cattle down to the Derby jetty for loading onto the boats. If you look outside the Shire Council offices in Derby you'll see a propeller mounted in concrete. It's from one of those boats, a relic of the earlier days. In the same way I think that old cattle trough is also a relic, yet very few people even know it's there. I doubt if the Shire Council or Shire President know about the older well at all. Yet this is the sort of thing that the tourists should be looking at. Maybe I should put a fence around it, claim it as mine and charge 50 cents a look. It hasn't deteriorated over all those years, the concrete looks just the same. (Derby Shire have made Myalls' Bore a tourist attraction, as Ivan thought - Ed.)

Some of those old fellas were what you'd call great cattlemen. People like Clancy Doggety, Eugene Hunter, Robert Flemming, Freddie Cox, Fraser Forgentus and my father, William Watson. I remember an old coloured bloke by the name of Billy Roberts. He used to get his two blue heelers, his riding horse, his pack mule, and his stock whip and away he'd go. He'd go right around Kalyeeda, and when he saw a mob he'd crack his whip and say, "Come on fellas, you know where you've got to go." It might have taken him three days to go right around that pastoral lease but, by the time he got back to the pool where he had the stock camp, the cattle would already be there. He had them trained to go to that pool. I've seen that with my own eyes.

Joe Griffin's cattle trough, Myalls' Bore.

But nowadays they use helicopters for the mustering. Personally, I wouldn't touch helicopter mustering with a 10 foot pole, because all they do is run cattle into the ground. It's not only the bulls and large beasts that get killed either. If an old cow is heavy with calf she's not going to run five or six ruddy kilometres, or whatever the distance is that they are trying to run them. Some of those stations try to run them for 10 kilometres! A beast isn't powered by an engine like a helicopter, it's made out of flesh and blood. Those that can't keep up with the pace just lie down and die from exhaustion. That's what it amounts to! And it certainly wreaks havoc with the calving season.

I don't like helicopters and I've said so from the word go. I even said as much when I was a foreman with the Main Roads. They are just a quick way of making money for the investors who buy into the stations. It's a quick way of stripping the joint. They weren't worried about the person who would be taking the place over. They didn't worry that he would have to rebuild the place. All they were interested in was a quick turnover on their money. Their mentality is: "Let's get in and buy the place, get what we can out of it, and move on."

When I left Mt Anderson in 1956, I left the place with 3,000 head of cattle, 26,000 head of sheep, and all the horses they needed. Good well-bred horses too. They even had some good race horses in the lot I left with them. Each rider generally had about four horses each, though I had about 11 of them. So you see, there were a fair number of horses. When I left the station, I left those horses there. The workshop too was always spick and span. All the materials we needed were stored on racks and we had all the equipment for jobs such as fixing the bores. We just had to pull the pipes and rods off the racks and book them out to the bore which needed the servicing.

But when we took over Mt Anderson around Christmas '84, we took over a run down joint, a dirty handkerchief as I call it. All the fences were down, there wasn't one left standing. Only four windmills were still pumping and one of those, the homestead one, was on its last legs. They had stripped the place something bloody terrible too. We had to go back to square one and start re-building the station. We didn't know where the breeders were, nor how many cattle we had. On top of that, the carrying capacity of the station seems to be less than half what it had been in my day. That's what we're up against.

It's true that very few stations have been bought for Aboriginal people, but the thing that I'm more worried about is the condition that those stations are in. The only stations Aborigines seem to get are the ones that have been run down or stripped. That's a very real problem for us. They were saying to us, when we started, it was a sit-down place, but that wasn't the way we looked at it.

The younger brother Harry and I decided that first of all we had to get the place cleaned up. And I tell you we were cleaning, and cleaning, and cleaning. It was a mess!

Abandoned station buildings, Lower Liveringa, 1988.

Mt Anderson station fuelling point, 1988.

We carried all the useless material out of the workshop. What we didn't throw in the rubbish heap we stacked neatly up on the ridge nearby. The floor of the woolshed was covered with a jumble of motors and all types of scrap, stretching from one wall to the other, and the place was littered with rubbish. We piled it all in an old iron trailer, which they had left there, and we stacked it out in the scrap heap.

The Aboriginal Development Commission paid $339,000 for Mt Anderson, and in my opinion they were ripped off. It was supposed to be a walk-on walk-off sort of deal, but a lot of things had disappeared by the time we took over. Even a lot of the cattle. The ADC people reckon that they counted the number of cattle on the property from an aeroplane; that's how thick they are! They couldn't see what brand was on them from an aeroplane, nor could they see what condition those cattle were in. As it turned out, they were in such poor condition that we decided not to muster them during the '85 season. They had been harassed so much throughout '84 already, by bushfires, helicopters and bull buggies. It looked as if the previous owners had used all those methods to strip the place. Maybe they didn't, but someone did.

Burnt out fencing on Mt Anderson.

It had only been freshly stripped too. After we took over, the fella from Camballin kept coming over annoying the brother. He kept saying to Harry, "I've been sent by the Government to check on you." He must have thought that we were idiots! I think that he was worried about his own skin, worried that we would find out that he was a partner in the whole stripping operation here. When I went into town next, I went to see the police and told them, "You'd better warn that fella at Camballin that he's not to go to Mt Anderson annoying my brother. Harry is the manager there now, and we don't want this fella sticking his nose in. I want you to chip him." Harry too told that fella not to come back again, or he mightn't leave the place.

We found out later that the police caught up with him eventually, but on another issue. You see he was stationed at Camballin, and when the Israeli mob took over the place they caught him hiring out the machines and pocketing the money. They fired him on the spot. But I think he had a lot to do with providing the machines and whatnot for stripping Mt Anderson. The previous owners had put fresh roads in from mill to mill. I don't know which grader they used but it could well have been the one from Camballin. Anyway, this bloke had the audacity to ask us to pay for all those roads they had put in. Of course, we could see that they had only been put in for the purpose of stripping the joint, so we didn't pay him a cent.

At first we didn't realise that all the windmills were worn out, because the majority of them were broken down as well. We took it for granted that all they needed was a servicing and we drew up our budget request to ADC on that assumption. But then we started to find out that all the bloody heads were worn out, the cogs, the drive wheels, the pinions and the arms. The whole box is worn in all those mills, due to the lack of servicing and maintenance over the years, such as failure to change the oil after the wet season.

That's one of the things I had to do when I was responsible for the mills here. I had to drain the watery oil out after the wet and put in new oil. Those big mills have a pump at the bottom which makes renewing the oil pretty easy. With the little mills you have to carry the oil up, and do your service while perched on top. How often had that been done since 1956? It had been neglected for a long time before we took over in 1984.

Those windmills had been spinning around with nobody bothering to control them. They've just spun, and spun, and spun for so many years that the ruddy heads are all worn out. When we tried to put them to work we found that the rods just couldn't lift the water. They just buckled up and the head fell off the towers. We tried to renew the head bolts but they just went "ping" and snapped off. I wouldn't ask anybody to climb up the Number 3 windmill now, what with the way the head is laying. We've got to wait now, until the head falls off completely. If we sent someone up there and they got killed who would be responsible then?

Bonzer lads

We get funding from ADC to cover vehicle and generator running costs, a few capital items such as fencing materials, and for the manager's wage. But there were no wages provided for the workers. When we tried to get money for their wages from ADC they said, "No, that's not our concern." They must have had the idea, when they bought the station, that we would all work for nothing, like we used to in the old days. An Aboriginal free labour issue all over again, working for a stick of tobacco, three feeds a day, or whatever. Otherwise, they must have thought that Harry was going to do all the work of getting the station back to being a viable operation by himself. We set out to help the brother anyway.

We've had some bonzer lads come through Mt Anderson, lads who've buckled down and worked for a while and then left because we had no money for them. I went down every different avenue I could think of, trying to get money for the boys' wages.

Eventually we got onto a young girl who worked with the Department of Employment and Industrial Relations. They're tied up somehow with the CES mob. (Commonwealth Employment Service - Ed.) She came up with a training program; so we took that out. It was all right while they were paying the full 100% of the wages. It was a different matter when it got back into our budget and we had to pay 60% of the wages. Of course that stuffed us up because we didn't have that type of money. It just wasn't allocated to us. We did get a bonus of about $3,000, but it wasn't nearly enough to cover the trainees' wages.

So that eventually broke up and we were back to where we started. We did get a lot of work done through a CEP project though. (Community Employment Programme - Ed.) The brother had a new windmill and tank put up, and a bloke came out and supervised the boys doing the job. We also had Frankie and his crew of three boys put up a fence all the way from one boundary right down to Pandanus Park. We felt good about that. Half of that job was paid for by CEP but we had to continue on after the grant ran out. That just left our own lads. Our sons and nephews got stuck with the job and had to finish it. It's been quite a battle.

The boys had to go into the CES office, where they were told, "Well, you've got to go and find work." They already had unpaid work at Mt Anderson. It's a sorry thing, because the fellas that want to get up and work get knocked in the bloody head and told, "No you can't get anything." Yet there are 6000 others sitting around this country who don't lift a finger; they just sit there and collect their dole. Now that's not the way to build a community. That's my point of view anyway. I don't know how others would see it. But we've got lads here who want to get up and make a go of things.

They put me in a corner and told me that I couldn't stay at Mt Anderson and still be on the dole. I thought to myself, "Well, that's pretty cruel; we've got a station here to run." It's not that I didn't want to do anything, I did. But at my age I couldn't go up to the Main Roads Department, or any of the other places where I've worked, and ask for my foreman's job back. They would say that it just wasn't on. They'd tell me, "Sorry, but you're not up to standard, you couldn't do it." And yet I've worked for 14 years with the Main Roads, starting off as cook and working my way up to a foreman. So that was the predicament I was in. Getting the rough end of the stick.

It finished up that I had a nervous breakdown over this issue. They told me that I wasn't allowed to help my own brother with the station. It really got me down, and in the end I got so bloody sick I had to have three lots of X-rays, blood tests and God knows what. I've been put off from being a worker now; they've put me on a pension. I had just wanted the wife to get enough money so that she could keep on living in Derby, and I would have been happy helping the brother at Mt Anderson. It didn't worry me that I had to rough it because I had lived that same lifestyle for many years.

"Sorry, she's gone to Melbourne."

In early '86 we took the truck down to Frazier Downs and bought 20 head of horses. We paid $100 a head for them, though when you take account of the fuel and tucker costs we probably paid out $2,500 in all. But it was well worth it. Once those horses were on the place those lads flocked back here, regardless of the fact that we couldn't pay them. We had all those horses broken in within six weeks. Eventually the lads went off again, but if we had the money to pay them we'd have no trouble keeping them here. Some of them are real stayers too. I want to see those young fellas that stick with us get something out of the station in due course. They're showing all the old fellas here that we can make a go of the place. All the old-time residents have shown their support for us too; they always come back here when we need them.

I've been upset about the wages for our boys, and I've gone through every avenue trying to get them something. We had a crowd visit the station to explain this new Community Employment and Enterprise Development Scheme. Apparently, the Social Security mob are willing to provide part of the wage, as long as we then lift it up to the basic wage for station workers. We went ahead and signed up on this new scheme. We don't really have much choice, if we want to get somewhere.

I don't know whether they want to see Mt Anderson and Looma getting up and making a go of things or not. It's easy to believe sometimes that they don't. The Looma community is our umbrella. There's no way in the world that we can get under that umbrella unless it's up too. They're our relations over at Looma, our flesh and blood, our bosses, and not for one minute should we say they're not. When we were trying to get this station, Looma got behind us, backed us up. We're put here by that mob because they know we belong to here; we're born and bred here to run the place.

Sometimes I think that they actually want to see us become a failure so they can say, "Look, Aborigines are just no good at running stations." In any business, you've got to have a flow of money in order to do anything. You can't say, "Pull up, we haven't got enough money to do that now," and still run a station properly. When it gets to the point where I have to tell the brother, "No, you can't do that job yet," it starts causing friction between us, because he's saying to me, "No. It's got to be done now." It's not my fault and it's not his fault. We need an easy money flow situation. If you're running a business, you've got to have that flow. If you don't, you're not going to get anywhere.

rooking Channel 16.3.83, Wet Season.

he Fitzroy River floodplain earns its name.

If they released our budget in July we could use it during the cooler months of July, August and September, when we can get the most value out of our workers. As it was, our money came after Christmas. What they expected us to run the station on, I don't know.

I rang the head of ADC in Sydney about it and the person there told me, "Sorry, she's gone to Melbourne." I rang Melbourne and the person there told me, "The commissioner's in a meeting, she'll have to ring you back." While I was waiting it occurred to me to ring a friend of ours who works in the ADC office in Perth. I got onto him, and he told me that the purpose of the meeting in Melbourne was to allocate funds. So I naturally thought that was it, the money would be coming through soon.

Then a fella rang me back from Melbourne and asked me what I wanted to speak to the commissioner about. I told him that I didn't need to speak about it anymore, I'd cleared it up. He said, "Well, you couldn't have got onto her anyway, because she hasn't arrived in Melbourne yet."

He must have thought I was born yesterday! "What were you worried about anyway?" he said. "Oh, we're waiting for our bloody budget," I said, "I was wondering why it was taking you so long." Well, he started going on about not having seen our budget request. "Why do you want it so early?" he asked. "It's not early!" I said, "We've got fencing to carry on with, we've got men here working, we've got accounts owing. I want to see myself right." So he said, "Can you wait for two weeks? You see, the money has to be released. It's passed but it isn't released."

Now you see the confusion. When he said it was passed I thought, "Oh well, we're going to get it now." I didn't realise it had to be released. Then we've still got to give it our acceptance!

This doesn't only happen on the telephone, it happens with paper. You write them a letter and it's important to you but there's a pile and something goes on top of it. That's a forgotten bit of material. One of them told me about it, he said we've got to keep reminding them. "It's the game we play," he said. I said, "I don't want games, I want movement."

Desmond Bedford, Mt Barnett.

We'll know that we're heading somewhere

Right through till now, we've depended on the goodwill of our creditors, such as the Shell Oil Company where we get our fuel, Elders who supply us with materials, and Woolworths who supply our groceries. They know us, and they know that we're a motivated mob who are trying to get somewhere. It hurts me to admit that we haven't got the money to meet our fuel, wire and materials accounts.

Those creditors might say, "Well, they're a bad mob; we can't let them book down here anymore." Of course that upsets us, for the simple reason that it puts us off balance. Shell and Elders are Australia wide, so if we lose the goodwill of their agents here, it won't just be this lot telling us we're no good; the whole of Australia will be saying it.

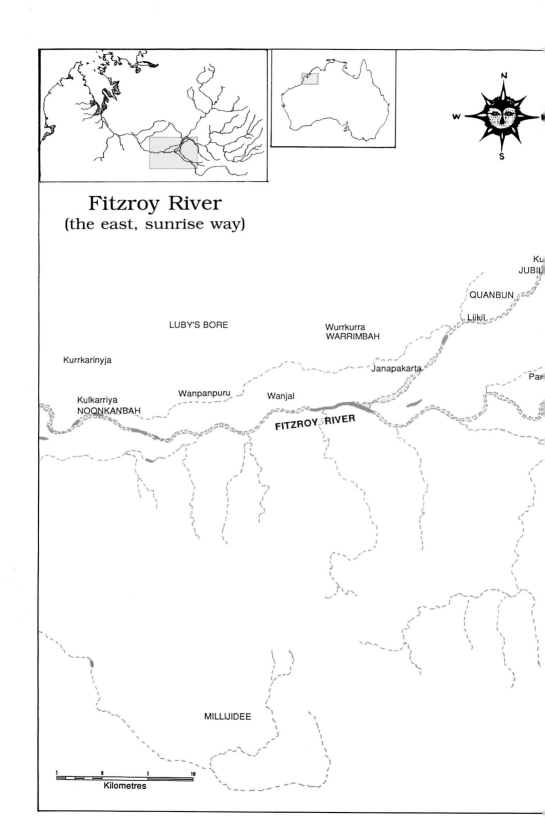

Fitzroy River
(the east, sunrise way)

Ku
JUBIL

QUANBUN

Liikil

LUBY'S BORE

Wurrkurra
WARRIMBAH

Kurrkarinyja

Janapakarta

Pa

Wanpanpuru

Wanjal

Kulkarriya
NOONKANBAH

FITZROY RIVER

MILLIJIDEE

5   0   5   10
Kilometres

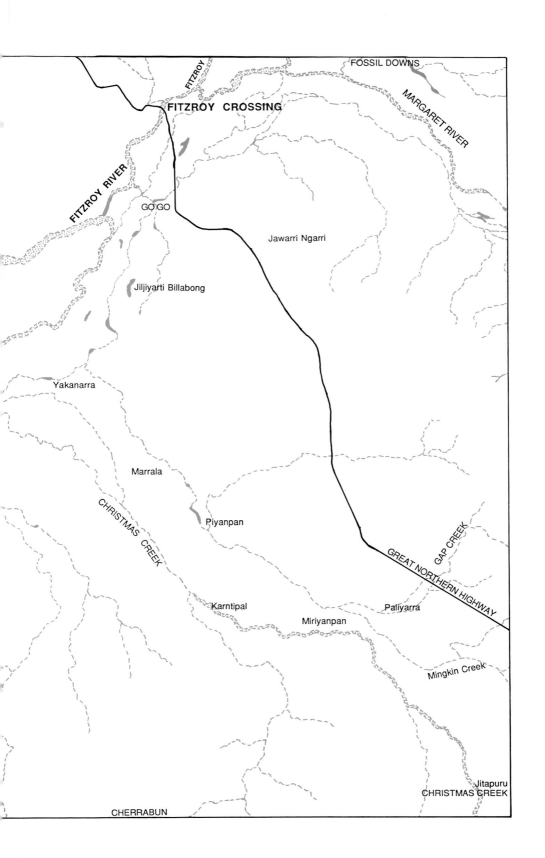

Fortunately, we were able to turn off 121 head of cattle in 1986. It was lucky that we did, because we didn't get any money from ADC between June and the New Year, despite asking them and asking them. It was only the money from those cattle that carried us through. To keep our creditors happy we had to go to them almost every day and say, "Look, we haven't got the money yet, we're still waiting." We didn't end up losing their goodwill, but it came that mighty close it wasn't funny.

Getting on to Christmas things started to get very tight. We were behind on two of the quarterly payments and it was coming up to the third. I wanted to know what was going on. ADC blamed their auditors for the delay. They told me the auditors hadn't given them their books and whatnot back. But the auditors were saying they couldn't give the books back until ADC supplied them with information they had requested. While all this was going on, we were up here trying to make ends meet.

They didn't seem to realise that they were cruelling things for us. We all felt a bit sore about it; even the Looma community felt a bit sore about it. When we've got to run back to our community asking for support it's pretty bad, because the community has to turn around and ask us, "What have you done with the money?" No problem explaining that; we've always been careful with how we use money. One thing I can say in ADC's favour, they have always allowed us to rearrange our budget so that we can get the top priority jobs done.

When we took over the station in Christmas '84, we discovered that both ADC and the Aboriginal Lands Trust had been made our silent partners. We've had quite a few meetings since then and we're still asking them about the role of the silent partners.

They're allowed to do what they want to do. But when we start to do something they always remind us that they're our silent partners, and that we should let them know what we're doing. But I don't see why we should be saddled with these two silent partners. Especially the Lands Trust; all they're doing is holding our deeds to the lease here. Why they're a partner at all, I don't know.

Standing, Adam Andrews, seated from left: Jimmy Green, Hughie Bent (hatless), Dingle, Bruce Wallaby, Har Marr, George Leopold, Billy Osc

166

Fitzroy Rivermouth in the Dry

This page shows the river as a thread running from the lower right into King Sound, upper left. The image was taken from Landsat satellite, 109 kms in space, on 2.9.80.

DEPARTMENT OF LANDS AND SURVEYS, WESTERN AUSTRALIA
117-072 DERBY   22050-01030   BAND 5 7
DATE:2/9/80   SCENE CENTRE: 17:20S   123:58E   SUN EL 42
DATE OF GENERATION:19/3/82   FULL SCENE

Fitzroy Rivermouth in the Wet

The Fitzroy River in flood. Willare Bridge. Image taken from satellite on 31.1.86. Images on this and the facing page supplied by courtesy of the Department of Lands and Surveys, Perth, W.A.

```
                DEPARTMENT OF LANDS AND SURVEYS, WESTERN AUSTRALIA
        110-072   DERBY   50701-01160              BAND  :2
        DATE:31/1/86
        DATE OF GENERATION:21/4/86
CROWN COPYRIGHT     FITZROY RIVER FLOOD  -  WILLARE BRIDGE                  R
```

I'll give you another example. Last year Elders offered to cover our costs for the muster. We were really encouraged by the confidence they showed in us. But someone in ADC's office in Broome at the time got really crooked about it. He thought that we had actually borrowed the money and had it in our hot little hands. Of course it was there if we required it, and that was all there was to it. In the end we didn't need to use it, so he was barking up the wrong tree. But he made sure he reminded us about this silent partner business.

Now if I wanted to know how to shoe a horse or spay a cow, none of those ADC fellas could tell me. I doubt if they could tell me how to fix a motorcar. They just haven't got that sort of practical knowledge. They only have one bloke up here with that sort of knowledge, and he's trying to do the job of nine people. That's their pastoral advisor, Bob McCory. He's a personal friend of ours. They gave him the job of going around and supervising all the Aboriginal stations, but there's no way in the world that Bob could do it all. He's only one man; how the hell is he supposed to cope with advising all those stations?

Now I'll tell you where the Government falls down. They've got a lot of separate bodies up here with no co-ordination between them, they're all out on their own limb. You say something to one department and they'll say, "No, that's got nothing to do with us, you've got to go and see such and such." There's nobody looking after the whole government issue up here. It looks that way to me anyway. There is no way any of those departments can tell me they do a better job than our own Resource Centres; no way in the wide world!

We've got to be able to administer our own money. I'm sure that would save on a lot of administration charges. We could appoint our own co-ordinator, and they could bring in their auditor when required. It would be as simple as that. When I needed money I would be able to sit down and say, "Listen, this is urgent. We've got to get this bullock paddock up before the wet. It's a priority. We've got 40 head of horses that we have to put in a paddock; otherwise we'll lose them all. It would also serve as a bullock paddock, so whatever we mustered could be put in there and shipped off early." The kartiya

170

are always telling us that we've got self-determination, but it hasn't reached that stage yet.

There has to be a priority for things. And board meetings ought to be up here, not down in Melbourne or Canberra. Then they could say, "Righto Ivan, I'll come out and have a look at what you want the funds for." They would be there on the spot. They could have a look and say, "Righto Ivan, fair enough." As it is we never see our so-called representatives. They don't come around; they don't sit down and talk with us. Or if they do they seem to think their moves are more important than ours, they say they're going to be here at eleven-thirty but they don't get here till twelve-thirty. Well that's an hour, in an hour I could be from here to Oodnadatta. We've got our duties, regardless that we're only a working plant, we've got to be here or there at certain times and it gets monotonous in the finish, waiting for hours for this fella and hours for that fella.

If we ever get the station back to how it was in the 'fifties, we'll know that we've gained ground. Then we'll know that we've fulfilled the hard part of our job. Fulfilled the job that Harry, John and myself, and the boys who have stuck with us, set out to do. I'd like to reach the point where I can say, "Oh, that windmill has broken down; we'll go out tomorrow and fix it." To have all the fences up and suchlike. Once we get that done, we'll know that we're heading somewhere.

Fitzroy floods, 1983.

Geike Gorge engulfed, Napier Range, 18kms from Fitzroy Crossing, 1983.

Go Go station, March 1983.

During the 'fifties and 'sixties different owners started taking over the stations, and those new people wanted to run their stations as they saw fit. They never asked for advice from the old identities of the Kimberley, they just went blindly ahead. You know, like those Americans who came out here thinking that they knew everything. But they proved at Camballin that they knew nothing about this country.

The Seventeen Mile Dam and the Barrage that they built has scoured a big section of the Fitzroy River frontage. From what they call Nurru Nurru Crossing today (it should be called Snake Creek Crossing) as far down as the Six Mile Creek on Liveringa. That whole area is just scoured to the billyo, because of the levee banks that they saw fit to put in. They were trying to divert the water from Seventeen Mile Creek/Uralla Creek/Lake Jocelyn/or whatever you want to call it, back into the river. But that's ridiculous, because it's the river that throws its banks and not the creek. The old road used to run between what we called Nine Mile Camp (Yalanganyja) and Six Mile Camp (Yita). But there's no road there anymore, it's just one continuous watercourse from one creek to the other.

The present river frontage isn't the river frontage that I used to know; it has really been cut to pieces today. We left Mt Anderson thirty-odd years ago, but we often went there fishing and so we were able to watch the frontage changing over that time. What with all the washaways and the formation of new channels, the change has been unreal. However, I'd say that the 1986 flood resulted in the biggest damage ever. Until recently, overstocking was the biggest cause of the soil erosion problem. It's something that the whitefellas never seemed to think about in the past. Basically it comes down to bad management.

I don't think we overstocked Mt Anderson at any stage while we were there. We actually improved the pastures there by introducing Buffel grass. I was amazed to see just how well it grabbed hold, though it hasn't done so well on the frontage. The Agriculture

Department are trying to do something about the terrible soil erosion situation we have along the Fitzroy River. They have started to set up test plots along the river frontage, and they're looking at a ten-year program of planting and measuring. Apparently they're going to play it by ear and see what becomes of this first lot.

But in my opinion, if this industry is ever going to climb again, we have to get better support from the Government. That's the major issue, no matter if its an Aboriginal station or a kartiya station. We have been getting help from the Ag. Department (Agriculture Dept. - Ed.) here on Mt Anderson, but it costs us $3,000 a year to get that help. They're hoping to regenerate the entire river frontage eventually, but they won't be able to bring back the beautiful plains that we knew. They're all scoured out now.

From Marr right down to Yukala used to be beautiful open country. Now it's not only scoured out, but it's got this prickly weed growing there, this Noogoora Burr. That stuff is starting to travel down the river now. It's very dangerous to stock, it gets in their intestine and does internal damage. Then there's this Pukaponius stuff; I've noticed it has spread from Marr right down to Yukala in places too now. (Pukaponius: more correctly, Parkinsonia - Ed.)

Whitefellas have been bringing in plants from all over the country and from overseas. They introduced the Kapok Bush too, and that's really gone wild up here. Apparently it is a fodder plant, with a good percentage of protein in it towards October/November. It kicked off in the Brooking Springs - Fitzroy Crossing area. You see it growing quite thickly there, and it grows thickly around Derby too. Native grasses such as Birdwood and Spinifex still make up the majority of the grasses around here, but I'm very concerned about our native grasses disappearing. We don't see much Pigweed, or Parrang Parrang, around here anymore.

Years ago we used to walk around in bare feet, but you can't do that nowadays. It doesn't matter where you go, you've got to have shoes on. You can't even walk over some of those places in thongs. Galland's Curse is the worst of the introduced weeds. It put the sheep out of this country. When those weeds started to take hold, people just couldn't shear the sheep. I've noticed that there's a grass growing on Six Mile Plain today which I've never seen before in my life. I don't know where it came from, but it's so coarse a ruddy buffalo wouldn't eat it. Actually it could be Buffalo grass. It's not really fit for anything to eat, its leaves aren't soft like grass, they're like sticks.

I remember when the Six Mile Plain was just a carpet of Pigweed with flowers of all colours. It was beautiful. You could look out from the Liveringa homestead across to Six Mile Plain, and you'd see a sea of colour - purples, reds and yellows. Even John can remember that during his day, though he probably would have only seen the tail end of it. That sea of colour was the indication that there was a big mat of Pigweed there.

The bullocks were really prime when Parrang Parrang, the Pigweed, was up. We'd always try to keep our bullocks on Six Mile Plain for a couple of days if we could. But the boss from Liveringa usually came down and told us to move on. The bullocks would be running around with that much fat on their backsides from eating Pigweed. It was very good cattle feed. The flats along the Fitzroy River used to be covered in it, but there's no Pigweed anymore, no matter where you go. The only place I see Pigweed growing today is around peoples' gardens. There was still quite a bit around in 1956, though not as much as back in the forties when all the frontage plains were just lush with it.

John and I were so taken with this last wet in '87 that we went for a drive to look at Willare. But there was something missing to my eyes, and that was the flowers of Parrang Parrang. You used to look out and see a nice green velvet of grass with that Pigweed growing all the way through it. So beautiful to look at, with all its different coloured flowers. Like a natural botanic garden. I miss that today, in my later years.

There's another reason why we miss that Parrang Parrang; our old people used to grind the seeds up with a stone and make a flour out of them. They have little black seeds or little brown ones, depending on which type of plant it is. You would never have tasted anything like the cake the old people made from Pigweed seeds. There's nothing that tastes as nice as that!

Highway raised above the Fitzroy floodplain at Willare - the China Wall.

Water over the main highway in March 1983.

Patja Honeychild (Yungar), Russel Bent, Anna Brown (child standing behind), unknown boy, Lucille Warmiya, Jinny Bent.

The ants are the main collectors of those seeds. If you got the plants at the right time you could just go along with a coolamon and knock the seeds in. Otherwise you had to pick them up from around the ant nests. That was the only place you could get them in any quantity. I remember one big old ant nest which no-one used to interfere with; it must have been there for years and years. But that area has suffered a lot of erosion in recent times, and those nests are starting to wash away.

It doesn't matter where whitefellas go, always the bulldozers, graders, and roadmaking follows behind. Actually, they're changing the country considerably. When they put roads over watercourses, it changes the flow of water throughout the whole area. And of course, that's how erosion starts. I hope those planners start waking up to themselves and take more notice of what they're doing.

The new all weather road across the Fitzroy River at Willare is a case in point. I reckon that new bit of highway is like a second Argyle Dam. It held back so much water during the 1986 wet, it was astonishing. I had to be boated out of Mt Anderson!

177

In all my life I've never known that much water to be in Gorge Creek. It backed up that far my brother had to come and boat me out in a dinghy. But that's not the critical part of it all. When the water receded it uprooted trees and washed out all the fences we had just finished putting up. It left debris clinging to everything. So before we could repair the fences, we had to pull the debris out. That gave us a double issue of work. It was disheartening to have just got the frontage fence up and have it washed away! Wasn't a big flood either, it was all just back-up water from this China Wall as I call it.

It should never have been built as it was! I spent a good 11 years with the Main Roads Department myself. That first section, from where the run-through was and right up to the first levee bank, should never have been touched. In my eyes that was a release path, because in a full flood that section never held any more than nine inches of water. So, if they hadn't built that section up, it would have released the river. But the way it's built will cause a lot of problems in years to come, you mark my words.

A channel of the Fitzroy, 1983.

It's got to follow its course

I predicted last year that I would see the Cockatoo Bridge out on it's own, and I did! That's what happened. In the same way, a few years back, I predicted that the Brooking Gorge bridge would be out on its own with all the abutment washed away. The same thing happened to both of them. Millions and millions of dollars went down the river because some bright blokes designed this in Sydney. I believe it was designed down there.

They don't know anything about the environment up here, nor did they bother to ask any old hands around town. They just went ahead with their plan. Well if that's engineering, I'd like to know how much more river frontage they're going to damage. They've damaged a lot already, even right back to where we are at Mt Anderson. All because of bad design!

After the water got so high they couldn't control it, some bright spark hit on the idea that they should release the river by dynamiting a section of the new road. So that's what they did. But that didn't just release the built-up water, it siphoned out everything upstream. It siphoned out big waterholes that generally hold water after a normal flood. They just weren't there after the '86 flood. It drained almost everything. It was a corruption of the whole river frontage! It gouged out many, many parts of our country.

The water got so high that it even went over Number 5 sandhill. Now that's going back five miles from Lower Liveringa, and I've never known water to go over that sandhill before. When the water was released it just scoured the whole area. This is nowhere near the river, it's right out between Mt Anderson and Lower Liveringa. You just want to see all the debris left around there, even up against the trees. We've got a billabong just down from the Number 5 windmill and there's debris around it. The floodwaters brought debris from hell knows where.

What that flood didn't siphon out it filled in with the topsoil that washed off the flats. It absolutely buggered up a lot of our pastures, our fodder grounds. They're all scoured out now. More damage was done to the frontage in that one year than in thirty-odd years preceding it. I took an Agriculture Department bloke out to Mt Anderson after that flood, and pointed out all the damage the flood had caused. But he wouldn't believe me; he wouldn't even believe that the debris on all the fences was left by back-up water.

With running water all the debris goes down stream, and it's gone, though some of it may get caught around the trees. It's the back-up water that leaves debris over everything. This bloke from the Agriculture Department had only been around a couple of years. It'll take him five or six years before he'll accept my practical knowledge. You get these fellas who are good on paper, but when it gets down to mother earth it's a different proposition. I've had the same problem on the Main Roads. I've had engineers come along who have just finished their scholarship, top engineers who've done their university and the whole issue, and when you get them out on the ground you lose them. They've got to go back and pick up their books. By that time I would have done another two miles.

We used to have fences running from the pindan to the river in my younger days, and we used to maintain those fences every year. We had that river frontage all divided up. But you couldn't put a fence there now, because you'd have no ground to put the fence on! The way it is now, by the time you get out of one scour you start getting into the next one.

There were once three channels to cross, going down through the ram paddock. Nowadays, as well as those channels, there's a whole lot of scouring between the main Snake Creek and the river. Our waterholes are starting to get filled in too. Such as Makaparlka, which was always a big waterhole as far back as I can remember. It's completely filled in now! When that bright spark got the idea of blowing the road to relieve the pressure, he caused more damage than he realised.

However, I know what the Main Roads Department is like. You can't tell those engineers anything; they're sixpence a dozen those fellas. They can draw plans that look good on paper, but when it gets down to practical knowledge those fellas are shot to pieces. You could lose them in one clump of bushes!

Now to my way of thinking, when they leave school, they should go out into the field and get the practical knowledge first. Then they could go and do their university later. That way they could put their knowledge and experience together. But doing it the other way round just doesn't fit in. In my time with Main Roads, I found out that whenever the engineers put something down on paper, you needed to work out what they were trying to do and change it for the better. That's the way I looked at it.

With the way they've designed that new "all weather" road, I reckon the Cockatoo Creek will finish up being a full face river before long. I really don't think those fellas know what they're dealing with. I was taught on the Main Roads that you can't compress water, but that's what they're trying to do at Willare. When I saw the way that section of road from Willare to Cockatoo had been constructed, when I saw the whole structure, it didn't look good to me at all. The situation had been summed up wrongly, and I couldn't see who was going to change it for the better.

I couldn't see the water getting away quickly enough, knowing the size of the catchment area. Especially if a freak rainfall in the Geegully Creek and Manguel Creek catchments added to all the water already coming down the Fitzroy River. The Fitzroy basin goes right back to Halls Creek, so there's a lot of country feeding water into the Fitzroy River.

They've even altered the structure of the levee bank! They're obviously trying to divert the water, but you can't divert running water very easily. It's got to follow its course. You can have all the theodolites you want to get your levels and whatnot, but when you're dealing with water it will make its own way.

The '86 flood ripped the creek near the Mt Anderson homestead to pieces. It was so bad we had difficulty getting our vehicles across. We needed a grader to fix it up, so we called the Shire and called the Shire again, but to no avail. We had arranged to get a mob of horses from Frazier Downs and bring them back to Mt Anderson on the truck. The Shire had promised that they would be there when we needed them but, as it turned out, there wasn't a machine available. So we went to see our next door neighbours at

Camballin. The fella we saw isn't there any longer unfortunately, he lost his wife and has gone away. He was an Israeli fella. It kind of touched me to think that an Australian had to go to a foreigner to get a bit of roadwork done.

Anyway, he lent me a front-end loader and his young son brought it over. That's the only way we were able to get the truck across that creek. Then we waited and waited for the Shire to make an appearance. The time for mustering came so we set to and mustered our cattle. We knew we would need to truck our bullocks out, so we notified the Shire again. I even notified them at the Fire Board meeting in Fitzroy Crossing. I said that I wanted it done on a certain date and they promised they'd be there. But they weren't.

It finished up that we couldn't load the cattle at our yards. We had to get the Agriculture Protection Board to bring out their portable yard, and put it up on the other side of the creek. Then two days after we'd done all that, the Shire came along and did the road. But even then they left it half done. The brother had to go and chip them about it, and they had to come back and do it again.

I want to finish this story by telling you a yarn I heard years ago from a kartiya fella. It's about the black ants and the white ants. If you look at the black ants you'll notice that they work out in the open. Now that's like the Aborigine, he does everything out in the open. But the white ants like to work under cover.

That's why they have to build their big anthills, their big castles or towers. They come out during the wet, cut the grass, and take it back to their big anthill. They work under cover and they want everything they build to be big. If you compare those black ants and white ants to Aboriginal and white people you'll see the truth of the comparison.

CHAPTER 6

All right, I'm looking for a job, I'll join you

Lochy Green

Mangala man (1925? -)

Tarpirl (Bush name)   Jangkarti (Skin name)

I was born on Myroodah station, or Kakinpala as my people call it, and worked there until I was a young man. Myroodah was a sheep station in those days and a bloke by the name of Harold Godbehear, or Old Gotby as we called him, was the manager. There would have been about 30 Aboriginal people living on the station when I was growing up, and all of them used to work; all except for the little kids. They just used to run around the camp. They never went to school in those days.

Some people would be doing the boundary riding, some would be doing fencing, others would be mustering and tailing the sheep. Some of the women would work around the station, keeping the place clean and cooking for the boss; others would work out in the bush with the men. The women would mainly do the cooking and cleaning around the stock camps, but sometimes they would do the same work as the men. Some women used to ride horses but most of the short distance musters were done by foot. The women used to walk along behind the sheep and often they had to walk many miles.

My mother used to work alongside my father when he was doing the fencing. My father would chop down the trees and cut the posts, and my mother would bark the posts and dig the holes. She also used to cut back the scrub to clean up the fence line. Often both men and women worked side by side at lamb marking time, grabbing the lambs and putting them up for the boss to cut their tails and knackers off, and earmark them. At shearing time my old man used to work in the sheep yards and my old woman worked on cleaning the wool. The boss used to put all the old women onto separating the wool and picking the seeds and other stuff out of it.

Upper Liveringa woolshed, 1916.

Violet Valley Aboriginal station, 1918.

I used to work at putting up the windmills and tanks, as well as mustering and droving the sheep. We'd bring them into the shed for shearing and then work around the yard, drafting, lamb-tailing, and even shearing sometimes. I used to shear the stragglers, you know, after the main shearing time had passed. I started work when I was just a young boy. I couldn't tell you when that was because I've never been to school. By the time I was fully grown we were working for one pound a month, but before that we didn't get any wages. We'd just get a shirt, pair of trousers, boots and hat. Some blokes got shaving gear and a mirror as well. The boss also gave all the working men a blanket and mosquito net.

If anybody on the station got sick or injured, Old Gotby would send them into the native hospital in Derby. They had a white hospital for the white people and a native hospital for native people in those days. The native hospital was on the site where the Numbula Nunga old people's home is now. Sometimes, when people were very sick, Old Gotby used to say, "It's too late to take them to hospital and I couldn't spare anyone to take them into town now anyway." We used to lose some of our old people on the station that way. They used to die.

186

I worked on Myroodah until that manager and I had an argument. So I left the station that same night with Peter Clancy, and walked into Derby. We camped the night on Liveringa property at Pangkulmanarn and got to Mt Anderson the next morning, kept on walking, camped the next night at Broken Wagon, and reached Yeeda station the following morning. There we met up with a motorcar coming from Lanji Bridge and got a lift up to Derby.

Peter and I got jobs then on Calwynyardah, working for Bill Henwood. Manjayi is the Aboriginal name for that place. We were still getting one pound a month. That was the standard wage for blackfellas in those days. Then Bill Henwood sent me with some race horses down to Broome for the races. After the nags had done their dash I decided to stop in Broome for a while. I was working in the soft drink factory there, still getting one pound a month. Eventually I got tired of that and shot through back to Derby. That's when I met this old kartiya fella by the name of Jack Huddleston. He told me that he was looking for men to make up a contract droving plant, so I said, "All right, I'm looking for a job, I'll join you."

His place was down near the bottom end of Noonkanbah, on the other side of Millijidee. They used to call it Huddleston station, but its Aboriginal name is Wulungarra. We built that place up from nothing. We built a bit of a house and some yards, put in a little windmill with a tank and trough, and dug a dam on one side. It wasn't very deep but it was good enough to water the horses. That was home for the drovers, with old Jack Huddleston as the boss.

We picked up our first mob of bullocks from Fossil Downs and drove them to Derby, loaded them onto the boat, went back and picked up a mob from Go Go. After we got rid of that lot we'd head straight back and collect a mob from Jubilee Downs. Usually took them in that order, and we only drove bullocks to Derby, not to Broome, at first. Derby had good shipping yards and a ramp while Broome had neither. The stock route to Broome was pretty scrubby and there wasn't much water between Nilapaplikan and Broome. Later on, after the Government put down bores along the stock route, people started droving cattle to the meatworks in Broome.

187

It was a really hard job droving bullocks in those days. A man had to be in the saddle from daybreak till night-time. There was both night work and day work. We'd drive the cattle during the day and watch them during the night. One fella would go to sleep while another watched the bullocks. We'd take turns watching them through the night, every night, for six or seven weeks.

We had three or four specially trained night horses in the droving plant. They were quiet horses, ones that weren't easily startled by strange noises or movements. With a good night horse a bloke could be asleep in his saddle and the horse would keep circling the mob. They knew their job, you didn't have to steer the night horses, you were just the passenger. You couldn't see in the dark like him. The night horses were always alert to the mood of the cattle, and some of them would even whinny or nod their heads to let you know the cattle were about to rush.

Once we got them to the big drovers' camp at Myalls' Bore, we'd sometimes have to hold them there for up to a week. It was a really hard day's work doing that! Keeping watch over five or six hundred head of cattle, all of them hungry for a decent feed. There was no yard there back then; we'd just have to watch them out on the plain with night horses. Sometimes we'd get to Myalls' Bore three or four days before the boat came in. Then we'd have to wait three or four days while they unloaded all their cargo onto the jetty. Once the boat was empty we'd take the cattle in. We'd work right through the night weighing them, dipping them, inoculating them, and running them through the cattle race and onto the boat. Often we'd have to work right through till nine or ten o'clock in the morning. All that for just one pound a month!

Sometimes we'd lose one or two bullocks on the road and sometimes we'd bring the whole lot in, without a single one missing. The station used to give us anywhere from four to seven killers to supply us with fresh meat for the journey. If we had any of those killers left over, we'd leave them at Myalls' Bore for the townsfolk. Jack Huddleston was a good bloke to work for. He was kind to the Aborigine. He never argued with the people or anything like that.

The only bad thing I would say about him is that he was very tight with the money.

He wasn't a rich man and he always seemed to have debts to pay off, so he never had any money left over. We had plenty of food and tobacco though, and he always made sure that he had plenty of whiskey. I worked with Jack Huddleston for four or five years. Unlike a lot of kartiya he would even take his turn on the night watch. He used to take the watch just before sunrise, and he'd start the cattle moving for the day; though sometimes he'd sleep in till the sun came up and cooked him out of bed.

In those early days the kartiya could do whatever they wanted, and a lot of them used to take Aboriginal girls for their sweethearts. They just used them and took off without them. Two of the head stockmen on Myroodah took black girls and kept them in their camp. That was Tim Lennard and Odo Frazer. Tim Lennard had my auntie's mother. Even Old Gotby the manager had an Aboriginal woman. Actually he had two wives, a white woman that he kept on the station, and a black woman that he had when he went out bush. But Old Gotby didn't have any kids by her. Maybe he was a dry bull, or maybe he used one of those prick jackets that the white men use. There was also a young fella by the name of Des Stuart who worked at Mt Anderson and had a black girl on Myroodah. That woman is old now and lives up at Numbula Nunga. That's four kartiya that I've seen with Aboriginal women on Myroodah station.

Dolly, Mary, Kitty, domestic workers on Cherrubin. Dolly was killed by a husband who thought her unfaithful. She died of septicaemia from Barramundi bones in the neck. Margaret Wells.

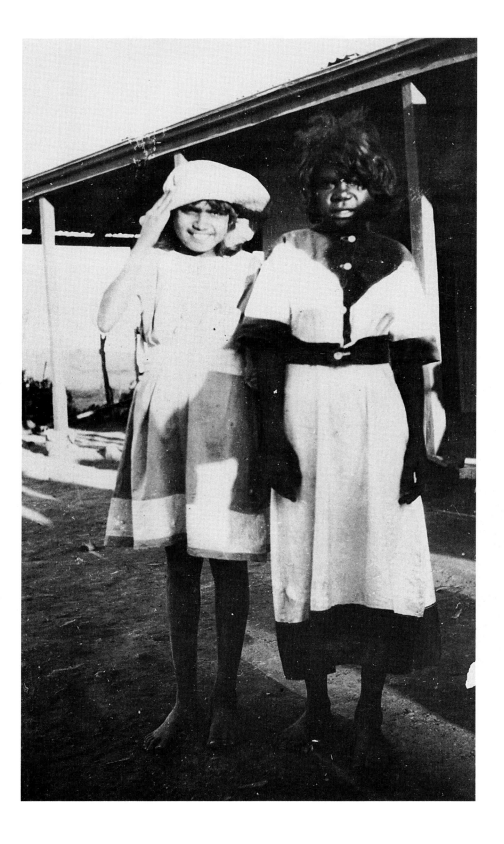

Myroodah used to be an important place during the Partukurru, or initiation time. That law business used to be held during the wet season, which was a holiday time on the stations. The managers used to let the Aboriginal people alone during that time, as long as they came back to the station when it was time to start work again. We used to set up our camp quite close to the stations, just inside the horse paddock. We'd collect our rations for the week, which was usually a bag of flour, some sugar and tea, a tin of fruit, and a stick of tobacco. Then the law men used to call people from all the other stations to come down for a big meeting.

Halls Creek corroboree, 1916.

191

Nindji-Nindji corroboree, imported from Victoria River to Anna Plains station, 1954-5.

The meeting ground was at the back of the Myroodah horse paddock, at a place called Jurrkarranyan. They used to put us young men right in the middle of all those people. We had to sit right next to the big law people and we weren't allowed to leave. We had to stay there and listen to those fellas, and they used to teach us the law the hard way. Those old fellas were hard people too. We were just like jailbirds, it was just as if we were in prison. We had to go out and hunt for those old fellas too, for goanna, kangaroo, fish and sugarbag. (Native honeybees' nests - Ed.) We would bring that food back and those old fellas would have a good feed and a good yarn, and then they'd start off the law business. We were there for nearly one month, doing that law. But the young fellas today haven't got that sort of fibre, they would just look at you and take off.

I'd like to see that blackfella law, that Tingnarri law, come back again. I'd like to keep it like it used to be. That's the sort of schooling we had! But the young people today are being schooled on the whiteman's side. They're learning kartiya ways. I know that all our people are still very strong about their culture, but they've got the whiteman's law hanging over them. So, they don't get much chance to teach the Aboriginal law. That's why those young people are able to just walk away from their old people. That's why they can get away with making trouble on the other side and then come back and make trouble in the whole family. The old people can't do anything about it.

Anthony Watson, Wayne Milgin, John Kibily, Campbell Yanawana, Anthony Yanawana, Darby Nungarin; Looma 1986.

Patrick Echo, good horseman, killed in a car crash, Warmun (Turkey Creek).

"White ants like to work under cover."

CHAPTER 7

I don't have any countrymen there

Peter Clancy

Mangala man (1934? -)

Kukari (Bush name)   Jangkarti (Skin name)

Everyone had to be able to ride

I was a proper bushman; I came out of the bush. I was born in the desert country, a long way south of Luluigui station. My father brought me up to Luluigui, or Kulakulaku as we call the place, when I was just a little boy. Before then, I had never even heard about whitemen. I didn't know how to say Yes or No. I came up with only the one language, my own. The one I was born into, Mangala.

The first kartiya I ever saw was a bloke by the name of Len McAlear. He used to live on Luluigui and he was always chasing after the Aboriginal people and trying to put them to work on the station. When we came to the station my father and I hid out in the bed of the nearby creek. Where the horse paddock gate is. We used to sneak into the station camp at night to get tucker. Well, one day the police came down and caught my father. Len McAlear tried to catch me but I ran away. He chased me right up the creek, but he didn't catch me.

I went back to our camp on the edge of the desert to tell my mother that the police had caught my father. But after keeping him tied up for a night they let him go, and told him not to keep sneaking around after tucker. They told him, "If you want tucker you can come back to the station with your family and work for it." The people at the station camp used to be punished if they were caught giving food to bush blackfellas. Father came back to our camp and gathered the family up, but he took us up to Jarlmadanga (Mt Anderson station) instead. John Watson's parents were his countrymen and he had come up to see them.

The second whiteman I saw was Canning Rose, the manager of Mt Anderson station. He was the first whitefella I was able to have a good look at. First I thought that he might have been a pulya (ghost), because he was as red as a baby kangaroo, or like a little new born baby. I remember arriving at Mt Anderson at Christmas time. That's when I first saw Johnny Watson; he was just a little boy at the time.

We left Mt Anderson and went over to Wungkarlkarra. It was what they called "government ground". They used to hand rations out from there. Kartiya called the place Udialla. The Government depot there was run for the Welfare mob by Mr Buckingham and Bert Brumby. There was another Welfare bloke there too, a Mr Bullen. He was the one who told me that I had to go and start work at Yeeda. As he was taking me there I was thinking, "I don't have any countrymen there."

I was worried about going there, but it was all right. I discovered that my sister Warbi, and brother-in-law Denim were working there. I sure was happy to see someone I knew.

So I started work there, at Yuluwaja, or Yeeda as the kartiya call it. Old Bulla, the head stockman there at the time, called me over and said, "You ride that grey horse over there." Well I had never seen horses before, let alone ridden one! I didn't know anything about horses! Never mind, I climbed on to the horse and it took off, heading straight for a tree with low branches. The old man was yelling out, "Pull 'im up, pull 'im up!" I was wrestling with the horse, trying to turn it. In the end I just jumped off. Old Bulla told me, "Never mind, you can stay back at the camp this time. Just work with Patjuwirri." So I started working around the station with a kartiya named Dan Senior, though known to us as Patjuwirri.

Not only did I not go mustering that year, I didn't even try to get on another horse. I already had some boots and a shirt back at the homestead camp, but Bulla had issued me with a new pair of boots, a shirt and the other things usually supplied to the stockmen, because he had intended to take me mustering. Then the wet season came and the Aboriginal station workers were allowed to go off on holiday. But I stayed around the homestead that year. I didn't try to go and find my father or my two sisters and brother. I just stayed with the side of my family I had found living at Yuluwaja.

Bridling up at Moola Bulla, 1910-18.

The next year old Bulla gave me a quiet horse and taught me how to ride it, taught me how to control it. I was all right then! Bulla was a good head stockman. He was an old man. He wasn't a kartiya; he was a "black bastard" like myself!

So that became my horse. You see, the thing was, everyone had to be able to ride a horse. Then, one day, Bulla said to me, "Righto, it's time you learned to gallop that horse." So I kicked the horse into a gallop and everyone got a laugh at me bouncing around in the saddle. You know, galloping the jackaroo way. Anyway, it took me a couple of months to learn how to handle that horse properly. When the next mustering season drew near, we started breaking in some new horses. The old man had me working with him, riding around the yards. He gave me quiet horses to ride at first, and then after a while he put me on a horse that was a little more lively. Then we went out mustering.

Bull terrier at the muster, Gibb River.

atrick Echo.

Wesley Kuldi, from Mowanjum, Jeffrey Dutchie, Johnny Malory, Noel Thomas, at Mt Barnett.

The first muster was on the eastern side of the river. We brought in about 500 bullocks, drove them up the road to Purrula (Derby) and helped load them onto the ship. We went back to the station and then went out mustering on the western side of the river. We did a circuit from the river to Kent's Bore, to Karrakurtany (Logue), to Nilapaplikan (Nilli Babbaca Well), to Mt Clarkson, and then back down to Pangngarri (Prior's Yard). In those days Pangngarri was an outstation for Yeeda.

We brought the bullocks in, took them up to Derby, and then went out mustering the country around Pangngarrikan (Fraser River). From the station camp, we would cross the river at Lanji and head up to Karrakurtany. We'd stop there for dinner and for a rest during the heat of the day. Then we'd ride up to Pangngarri and camp there for the night. Next day we'd make Mt Clarkson our dinner stop, and we'd camp the night near Kurrupirrin Creek. From there we would ride straight through to Pangngarrikan. We spent a long time mustering that country.

When we had enough bullocks mustered, we'd take them back to the station. That's where I learnt how to throw bulls and bullocks. I learnt all about cattle work and handling horses at Yuluwaja. I worked there for four years, and in all that time the station never paid me. They supplied me with boots, shirt, trousers, a blanket, some calico and a mosquito net. But I never got any money, not one black penny! I got my first pay from a contract drover, after I helped him drove a mob of cattle from Yeeda to Myalls' Bore. He gave me 10 bob. The other more experienced drovers got two pound. The young fellas, like me, just got 10 bob.

Myroodah station quarters, 193

"You'll have to go and sleep somewhere in the mud!"

After that, I left Yuluwaja and started mustering on Mt
Anderson. My father, Narlpuyiti, was working there at the time too.
I hadn't seen him for four years. After a year working at
Jarlmadanga for two pound a month I went back to Yuluwaja and
started getting four pound a month. All the stations had started to
pay good money by then, they were all paying their Aboriginal
stockmen four pound a month.

Then I got fed up with working at Yuluwaja, so I took off and
went down to Kakinpala (Myroodah station). On the way there I
stopped off at Pintinyin (Liveringa station) and had a good look
around. When I got to Kakinpala I just started hanging around, I
wasn't interested in taking on any work. But then Lochy Green
reported me, and they put me into a job. Lochy wanted me to work
with him as an off-sider to the windmill bloke, Mr Widgee, or Comet
as he was called. Comet put me to work straight away, and then he
went along and told old Gotby that he wanted me as one of his off-
siders. He had to pull up the casing on a big Southern Cross windmill
at Hart's Bore, and he needed extra help. So that's how I came to start
work at Myroodah.

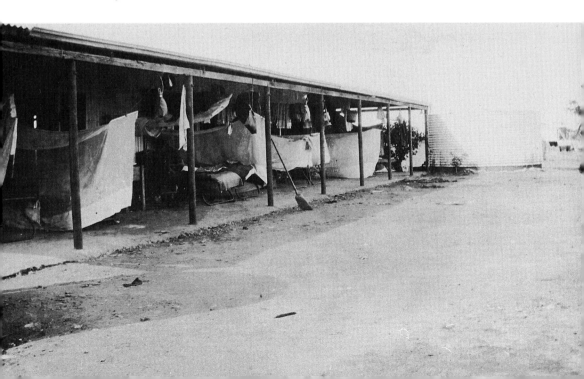

Windjana Gorge, Napier Range.

Mt Anderson.

I worked there for two years until Lochy fell out with the manager and took off. So I took off with him. There had been a lot of winter rain that year and there was no housing provided for the Aboriginal people. Everyone had moved into the shearing shed and the saddleroom, but there were a lot of people and there wasn't much room. We went over to the shed like the rest. We wanted to camp there too, but old Gotby came up to us and said, "There's no more room for you in the shearing shed, there's too many people camped in there already. You'll have to go and sleep somewhere in the mud!" That's how we fell out with old Gotby.

So we got our blankets and other stuff, and we took off from Kakinpala that night. We crossed over the river at Myroodah Crossing and camped the night at Pangkulmanarn, which is near Jirrip on Liveringa country. We arrived at Jarlmadanga the next afternoon, and camped there for the night. The next morning we headed on to Palkanjirr, and ended up camping at Jinarrkan that afternoon. We reached Liwan the next morning, and arrived at Yuluwaja in the afternoon. We had our supper there and then got a lift in a motorcar right up to Derby. We had seen some half-caste fellas fishing at Lanji Crossing that morning, and they ended up giving us a lift.

While we were in Derby a bloke called Bill Henwood came up from Manjayi (Calwynyardah station). He was looking for workers. Manjayi was a sheep station at that time. Anyway, we got a lift down to Manjayi, and started working there on six pound a month. I worked there for two years and then I went up to Paninypukarra (Paradise) and started getting seven pound a month. It was a sheep station there too, an outstation of Liveringa. Old man Kim Rose was the boss of the station and Henry Gooch was the manager of Paradise. I worked there with Budi, Wimirrin, Midi, Lukamaraji and old man Bumbi for three years. Those fellas were all Aborigines; Goochie was the only kartiya there.

Then, while I was still at Paninypukarra, my father died. It would have been about 1953. So... I left there, and went off by myself for a while to mourn. In Aboriginal law people in mourning aren't allowed to eat meat, except for fish and other things that live in water. We usually do that for about a month but some people keep it up for years.

After a while a kartiya brought me into Derby and left me there. That's when I met this fella by the name of Norm Buckle. He wanted me to go and work with him on Cherrabun station, putting up windmills. So I went there and worked for him, but he didn't pay me anything. All I got for the work I did was some meat and bread. He robbed both me and another bloke, Marna Hairpin, of the wages that were due to us. So we finished up that job and went to the races in Fitzroy Crossing.

After the races had finished, I went down to Kulkarriya (Noonkanbah station) and started working for old Duncan Beaton. I was getting eight pound a month, and I worked there for three years, mustering and boundary riding. Me and Barney Jilayi were the boundary riders. First I stayed at Wurrkurra (Warrimbah outstation) and worked the country north of the Fitzroy River. Then Barney and I went down to Millijidee, and started working around there. We were building yards and doing all the other jobs that needed attention. After that I went back to Wurrkurra for a while.

I made my first trip to Broome then. Mulamulu Friday and I got a lift in a motorcar down to the Broome races. The bloke who had taken me went back to Noonkanbah without me, so I decided to get a lift to Derby in another motorcar. That's where I met up with the boss for Kungkarakarta (Jubilee Downs), a bloke by the name of McNamarra. He told me they needed a windmill worker at Jinjirlkan (Nerrima station) and offered me a lift there. So I went down to Jinjirlkan and worked there for six months. Johnny Watson was working there too at the time. That would have been around 1962. After six months there I went back to Paninypukarra for a while and then went back to Broome. I liked it in Broome.

My brother, Michael Mowandi and I got a few months' work in Broome as builders' labourers. We were helping with the construction of the new Broome Police Station. When that job was finished I went back to Derby and then down to Kakinpala (Myroodah) again. My son, Jungkurra, was due to be initiated that year. So I worked on Kakinpala until the wet season came and the stations broke up for holidays. That's when all the law business goes on. People used to gather on Kakinpala from all around. A lot of people came up from Bidyadanga (La Grange) that year; and after it had finished I got a lift in the truck with them back to Bidyadanga.

I camped at Bidyadanga for a couple of nights, and then I went down to Yawinya (Anna Plains) and started working for Mr Fred Wright. He was the boss there but the bloke who actually ran the camp was the head stockman, an Aboriginal fella named Mr Tarlun. The old money had finished by then, they had brought in the dollars. I was getting $192 a month, which was good money in those days. I worked at Anna Plains for about a year and then I went down to Ngalji (Mandora station). They had both cattle and sheep there, so I had to work them both. I worked there for about two years and then I went back to Anna Plains.

That's when I broke my knee, and after that I could no longer do stockwork. They just pensioned me off then. I didn't get any worker's compensation. I got nothing at all! I think the station should have paid me some compensation for that injury, but I got nothing. I'm still limping around today because of that injury.

Fitzroy Crossing ceremony, 1986: Michael and Trevor Chessnut, twins, with leaves in hair as initiates, Fred Purti
with hand raised, singer and MC.

The cave pool refuge, Mt Anderson.

CHAPTER 8

We know this country

John Watson

Nyikina man (1940 -)

Tatika (Bush name)   Jakamarra (Skin name)

He didn't say whether we could eat together

I was born into the pastoral industry. I grew up working sheep, horses and cattle. All my family worked on the station, mustering, branding, fencing, yard-building, digging dams with donkey teams, breaking in horses, building windmills. My mother and the other Aboriginal women looked after the gardens and the boss's house. They did all the cleaning and cooking, both for the boss and for the workers. Even the kids used to work, helping in the garden and that sort of thing.

From the early days Aboriginal people were forced to work on the stations. The police issued the station managers with permits to work the Aboriginal people and to take charge of their welfare. That happened right across the Kimberley. All the stations came to depend upon cheap Aboriginal labour. The Aboriginal people knew they were being exploited but they didn't have any choice. Then, during the 'fifties and 'sixties Aboriginal stockmen started pushing for better wages. They didn't realise the drastic effect it would have on their lives.

When the equal wage decision was handed down by the courts twenty-odd years ago, the Aboriginal people were forced off the stations. It had very far reaching effects, from one end of the Kimberley to the other. Hundreds of people were forced to leave the stations they'd grown up on, and to live under appalling conditions in town reserves. Those station managers just came out and said, "We can't afford to pay you the basic wage, and we can't afford to keep feeding you. The Welfare mob have a lot of money for you to live on in the town. So, pack up your camp and start walking."

The next thing we knew the stations had brought up white stockmen who didn't know anything about the country they were to work in. Quite a few didn't even know how to work cattle. The Aboriginal people had that knowledge and experience, but they were pushed off the stations. We shouldn't forget that the mustering of cattle by aeroplane and helicopter started from that time, as did the use of bull-buggies to run the cattle down. The decline of the cattle industry, which is so obvious today, can be traced back to that fundamental change in how the stations were run.

The Department of Community Welfare took all those displaced Aboriginal communities strongly in hand and settled them onto town reserves. But then their big failing was that they didn't have the courage to say, "Look, the Aboriginal people want to settle out in the bush. They want to maintain their own communities and have charge over their children's education." For the same reasons Aboriginal people are trying to re-establish their communities out in the bush today, despite the many difficulties.

On the stations we had three feeds a day. We got no pay, but at the time we didn't worry about that. We had our daily routine all mapped out; it was the habit of the people to get up early in the morning, and do this job and that. Today, most of those people have nothing to do. It saddens me to see them going down to take up where they left off the day before; you know, with drinking and carrying on, getting thrown in jail and getting into trouble.

I remember the day when Aborigines were given the right to drink alcohol. I was young, and when I looked at it I thought it was a good idea. I remember a local Liberal party politician, Alan Ridge, announced to the Aboriginal people, "We have equal rights now; we can sit down and drink together." He didn't say whether we could sit down and eat together! I think drinking rights came in at the same time as the equal wages, and I suppose it referred back to that - equal rights, equal wages, equal drinking rights.

I've been waiting a long time to see things change, but they haven't really changed. You know you can go to the Government people, you can go to Parliament House in Canberra and ask, "What are equal rights?" But I don't think they'll give you an adequate answer. So, the Government said they had given us equal rights, and we no longer needed a licence in order to drink in the pub. But alcohol has created a lot of problems for my people today. Every Aborigine who drinks would have a police record a mile long. That's really bad. I mean to say, alcohol has busted up a lot of my people, a lot of marriages and a lot of family relationships. It's not a problem which is confined to Aboriginal people. I know alcohol has done a lot of damage on the whitefella side.

One answer to the problem may be to set up alcohol rehabilitation centres, but there is another answer from my point of view. I was the chairman of the Kimberley Land Council for six years, and I know that a lot of people want to go back to their own country. People from all the language groups have stood up in meetings and spoken strongly about that. They want to go back to their own land so they can overcome the problems of alcohol and violence and so they can give their children a better chance for the future.

Their country may be on vacant crown land, it may be on a stock route, or it may be on pastoral leases. But it's very straight forward from my point of view. Now, that answer to the alcohol problem hasn't really been talked about in Parliament, not in Canberra and not in Perth.

Sandra Brooking, Susan Chiganoo (at counter), Bruce Wallaby, Terry Clifton, Ted Beharrel, Junjuwa Community Office, Fitzroy Crossing.

I must say that 'land rights' is not a very good word; it's a word that politicians have made dirty. Ten years ago the Federal Government decided that land rights should be granted to Aboriginal people. It was a word that we could play with, but it's a whiteman's concept and a whiteman's phrase. I've been thinking this for quite a long time, even while I was involved with the Seaman Land Rights Inquiry. I say, "Aboriginal people want to go back to their own country." In my opinion, governments shouldn't presume to grant those lands to those people, because in Aboriginal law they already own it and belong to it. Instead, the State and Federal Governments should be offering those people support so they can go back to what is their own land. After all, they've been here 40,000 years and they have the law and culture to that land.

The town reserves don't provide a very good living situation, whether it's in Derby, in Fitzroy, or in any of the other towns here. It's not a good environment in which to bring up kids. But if those people were to move out bush, they would need to have a two-way radio, a water bore, an ablution block, an emergency airstrip, and a decent access track.

Junjuwa, Fitzroy Crossing.

Mary Anne Downs, Trixie Shaw, Dolly Snell, countrywomen now in Fitzroy Crossing.

We have raised these matters on many occasions with people in the Government who call themselves experts at understanding Aboriginal people, but they have yet to give full support to those people who want to move back to their country. They hadn't in 1986 to the people who had already moved back and set up communities in places like Yagga Yagga, Ngarantjartu, Ringer's Soak, Sturt Creek, Jalyirr and suchlike.

Those outstations need ablution blocks, and not all of them have plenty of housing, like Ringer's Soak now. Some of them haven't got one decent house. They need a place where they can put their radio away from the weather, and where they can keep their stores dry. They're often sleeping on swags out in the open because that's all they've got.

One community I went to even had their radio taken away from them! It was on loan from the Department of Community Welfare, and one day the welfare people came out and said, "We're going to take our radio back." I don't think that should have happened. What should have happened was for DCW to say, "Look, we want you to put this in the next submission you write. You should say that you want another radio so that you can keep in contact with DCW and with the Resource Agency. Tell them that at the present moment you're using one on loan from Community Welfare." You know, something like that should have been done.

Communities can be pretty hard to get to, more than a hundred kilometres from the nearest town over rough roads and sand dunes. Some roads have been so badly scoured by erosion that you only get through with a four wheel drive vehicle. Often those communities don't have a decent vehicle. That's why a two-way radio and a good airstrip mean so much. The flying doctor could easily mean the difference between life and death for those people.

They set those communities up because they wanted to teach their children all the skills their parents once taught them. They have the law to that country, they have the culture to that country; and they want to pass them on. Government people don't always understand that. They think they understand us, but they don't really, not yet. Do they support us forming our own organisations, such as the Land Councils? We don't have an organisation like the Pastoralists and Graziers. My brother Ivan thinks we shouldn't have a separate Aboriginal Cattlemen's Union, and I agree with him. In his view it's an industry we should all be involved in and we should be able to join them. He put it this way, "If there's a meeting of European cattlemen, I'd like to be there to let them know that we're just as good as they are. Let's get on with the job, we're looking at a meat industry here and we're a pastoral lease owner now."

Patrick Echo, Eddy McCoombe, Mt Barnett.

I got into an argument over all the unfulfilled promises made to Aboriginal communities from the Pilbara across to the far north Kimberley. This official had come up to Derby in July '84 and attended a big meeting at which a lot of promises were made. A number of those promises still hadn't been fulfilled 10 months later when he came up to attend a meeting of the Western Desert Land Council at Well 33 - Kunawaraji.

Shane Munro, Larry Green, at Junjuwa.

So I stood up at that meeting and put him on the spot. I thought that as a big man in the Department of Aboriginal Affairs, he was supposed to be answerable to the Aboriginal people. He had said as much himself. Mind you, I was on the Federal Government's payroll at the time; I was working for the Kimberley Land Council on money allocated by DAA. But when the KLC's next allocation came through I discovered that my position was no longer funded. So it seems that straight talk doesn't go down very well with those government people. I don't think it was a very fair thing to do! When they cut your funding off it's like cutting your legs off, so you can't walk; or like cutting your tongue off, so you can't talk.

It's always the politicians who have the say as to what will be carried out in whatever area. But it's obvious that the local politicians, the people who run the shire councils in the Kimberley and elsewhere, don't want to see the Aboriginal people elected as councillors. In 1985, when the Aborigines of the Kimberley were given the right to vote in local government elections, quite a few Aborigines stood as candidates.

There was a deliberate campaign to keep Aboriginal representatives out of the councils. That campaign extended from the non-Aboriginal candidates directing their preferences away from the Aboriginal candidates, to scare mongering about Aborigines gaining control of the councils. One local newspaper editor who was busy promoting that scare campaign had only recently come into this country. But the Aboriginal candidates were born in this country, and had spent most of their lives here. They were keenly aware of the many frustrations felt by Aboriginal communities and they were trying to make the Kimberley a better place for Aboriginal people. It seems that very few white voters wanted to see Aboriginal people elected to the councils.

Those candidates weren't given the benefit of the doubt, they weren't given the chance to do something for their people. We thought we knew some of those kartiya, but we were surprised to see the racism that emerged during that election campaign. Obviously we've still got a long way to go, but nevertheless the time will come.

I don't criticise the Aboriginal Affairs organisation. What does make it hard for them is they're bound by the rules too, there are certain things that they've got to carry out, and they're worried if they don't do it right and check back with someone, they'll cop it. They're bound by that law, over their shoulder, that rule book, they have to go square by that. I know the frustration that people get into, I had that situation myself. These government officers who are put out in the field, they're under that rule, given by the top people, the Canberra people. They can only argue on what their rule book says. If they didn't argue they'd get into trouble, lose their job. It is bureaucracy.

While I was the chairman of the Kimberley Land Council, I called several general meetings a year. Quite often I invited politicians and high-up people from government departments to attend one of the meeting days, so that they could explain their policies and initiatives. Now these people tend to speak a high English which is often very difficult for my people to understand. So when they've finished speaking and they ask if anyone wants to speak or ask a question, it's usually the people who've had practice talking with government people who speak. The others are usually too shy or too intimidated.

Bantam Jutumarra, Junjuwa. Delson Stokes calling riders at Noonkanbah rod

But then we turn around and find out that our good strong speakers are being labelled as 'activists'. That sort of thing really annoys me! Those strong speakers are Aboriginal people; they understand the Aboriginal way and culture, and they try to speak up on behalf of the old people. But the next thing we know we hear some politicians saying, "Aboriginal activists are getting in the way and causing problems for Aboriginal communities." They think Aboriginal people just want things to revert back to how they were years ago, and they try to slate anyone, like myself, who says otherwise.

You hear some politicians say that we should try to work together with the rest of the Australian community but how can we work together when we can't get our message across? If we can't communicate face to face we have to try to get our message across in other ways. One way of doing that is through this book, but the language problem will always be a major stumbling block.

Another very real problem is that Aboriginal people, by their own customs, can't make decisions straight away. They are always worried about undermining the next person. They are always obliged to listen to those people who have the right to speak for the country in question; or to anyone else who has clear speaking rights. If that person wasn't at the meeting then they couldn't make a decision straight away.

Colin Shaw, John Charles, Fred Purti, a winter meeting at Junjuwa, 1986.

That's why there is often a bit of a hold up, and that's the sort of thing that the government people don't understand. Nor most of those other white people who come up here to consult Aboriginal people on their various plans and proposals. If they want us to live together and share things, then they have to accept that some decisions take time.

Aboriginal people have been responsible for working cattle, sheep, horses, and men, right through the Kimberley. We've been good workers too. We know this country, we know the environment, we understand its character and its history. We are the people of this country. We should be given an equal say in any development proposals, and we should be given a more equal say in the running of stations.

There are about five dozen stations in the Kimberley, and only eight are in Aboriginal hands. That's Carson River, Frazier Downs, Billiluna, Bow River, Dunham River, Pantijan, Noonkanbah and Mt Anderson*. Those stations are just places that Aboriginal people are leasing from the State Government. We just have the responsibility for working them and trying to better them. We're trying to get them back to the same standard they were at before the Aboriginal people were forced off them.

The old people who are back on those stations now were reared up there; they're the people who helped build those places. I'm not just talking about Mt Anderson, where I was born; I'm talking about other stations as well. We want the Government to sit down and really negotiate with us. We want to get better rights to those stations so we can build them up for our children.

The Government has a job to restore something to us for taking away our land and interrupting our culture and our language. Even in my time, Aboriginal children were being taken from their parents and sent away to one or other of the mission schools or government institutions. My younger brother and I were nearly taken away to Moola Bulla. Had that happened, we wouldn't have known our parents; we wouldn't have even known where we had come from. We would have been robbed of our language and culture just like all the others.

* That was in 1988. Since then the following stations have been added to those under lease to Aboriginal Communities in the Kimberley of Western Australia: Carranya, Doon Doon, Gibb River, Glen Hill, Kupatiya (Bohemia), Kupungarri (Mt Barnett), Lamboo, Louisa Downs, Millijidee, Mt Pierre, Tjurabulan (Lake Gregory), Yarrangii (Leopold).

Only a few made it back

I never got a chance to meet my two eldest brothers because they were taken away before I was born, when they were only 9 or 10 years old. My sisters and another brother were sent away to the Catholic mission school at Beagle Bay. My parents had no say in that, it was government policy. Aboriginal children right round Australia were forcibly taken from their parents and placed in institutions. The police could take away any Aboriginal child with a bit of colour in them, any kid with a bit of white blood in them. If they were taken away, it was often the last time their parents and relations saw them. It was a very sad thing!

When it looked like the younger brother and I were going to be taken away as well, our parents got talking and decided that they weren't going to part with us. So, whenever a police party came out to Mt Anderson they sent us off into the bush; sent us down to our father's and grandmother's country with some old people.

That's why I'm able to speak my own people's language and several other languages. My sisters and other brothers missed out on that. Of course they can understand what's being said in language, but they can't speak it very well themselves.

Violet Valley, 1910-18.

gle Bay Mission, 1950s.

The police used to ride right down into the desert to capture Aboriginal people and bring them back to work on the stations. If any of the station owners or managers told the police that they were short of workers, the police would bring some of their captives back to that station. In those days the police were also the official Aboriginal Protectors. They used to give the station managers a permit to hold them on the station, and to work them as they saw fit. Even if those Aboriginal people had parents and friends on a neighbouring station, they wouldn't be allowed to go there without the manager's permission.

If any of them ran away from the station the manager would send for police to round them up and bring them back. Or, if they were considered to be troublemakers, the police might send them off to prison. Though sometimes the police decided to kill them, and get rid of them that way. In those days the police were a law unto themselves; they had nobody else over them. Most of them were the biggest rogues going too!

Aboriginal people were dragged all round the Kimberley by the police and the Native Affairs people. That's why there's been such a big mix-up in our languages and our people. I know that sort of thing continued up until 1952. It was all right for some people; they

221

got married and settled down in the places they were sent to. Some of them had relatives who had also been sent there, but most of those people did want to come back and the police just wouldn't listen to them.

They had sent those people away for good, since they didn't make any provision for their return. Some of them tried to walk back but most of those died or were killed on the road. Only a few made it back.

Some of those people had young families too. When their children grew up they were told, "Your father was taken away by the police and never came back." But you know, when we tell the Government about the wrongs they have done to our people, they don't want to listen. They don't want to be reminded of those things. They say we're bad people just because we're arguing with them.

I think the Government should accept responsibility for the wrongs the police committed against the Aboriginal people. I've been talking to some of the old people and they've told me about some of the murders and massacres which they know of. The police used to have a number of camps around the Kimberley. Those camps served as half-way bases from which they could make sweeps through the bush. There's the well-known ruins of one such camp up near Windjana Gorge, Lillimooloora, where Pigeon shot those policemen. There was another one down on Luluigui station at a place called Karpali Nyurtany. But the main police camp in this area was on a hill between Upper Liveringa and Mt Anderson stations, which the Aboriginal people call Jirrip. It overlooks the stock route and the old sheep yards at Pangal Pangal.

The police used to use Jirrip as a base for their sweeps through Luluigui (Kulakulaku) and Myroodah (Kakinpala) stations. You see, it was too far for them to go back and forth to Derby, since it used to take two days to travel from Jirrip to Derby on horseback. When the police had rounded up all the people they were after they would walk them back into Derby. At the same time the Fitzroy Crossing police were also sending out patrols to round up groups of Aboriginal people, and they used to use Jirrip as the half-way camp for the journey into Derby with their captives. The police used to ride along on horseback and their captives would walk along behind in chains. They used to chain their legs and hands as well as putting a chain around their necks.

When they got them to Jirrip they used to chain the trouble-makers up, with their legs spread out around a tree, and flog them with a green stick. The old people tell me that the police also used to get their trackers to flog them, while they stood by with their guns ready. They made them do that to their own people! Then, when the poor fella's back was all cut up from the flogging, they'd tell their trackers to rub salt into the wounds. Those people used to scream and carry on, and some of them even used to die. But of course there's no official record of any of this happening.

If any of those police trackers refused to do as they were told, if any of them tried to accuse the police of committing a crime, they would get beaten up. If they still refused to do as they were told, then they would be shot dead. From what the old people told me, some police trackers were shot for just that reason. Not many of the old people who witnessed these things are left to tell their story, but I'm sure that the things they've told me happened all over the Kimberley.

Halls Creek, early contact, early 20th C.

The other police camp at Karpali Nyurtany used to deal with the Mowla Bluff/Ngi Ngi area which lies to the south of Mt Anderson, up the Geegully Creek. I was taken there in 1959 by an old fella who showed me the remains of a lot of dead people. There were no real skeletons, just bits and pieces of bone laying here and there, and there was a patch of soil that had been made black from the fat of all the people who had been burnt there. That old fella who took me there told me the story of the big massacre which happened there. Hundreds of Mangala people, my father's people, were murdered by the police at that place.

I'll tell you how it happened. The story goes back to an old Aboriginal fella by the name of Gunna Wyatpan who went off with his relative's wife. A few years later the people caught up with him and put a spear through his leg. That was the proper punishment according to their law. Anyway, somebody else came along the track, picked him up and treated his wound. He came out of it alive, but apparently he decided that he'd get his revenge on those people. So, a few years later, he went along to the police station in Derby and offered himself as a police tracker.

Derby police mounting yard, 1920s.

evil's Gap, Napier Range.

indjana Gorge heights.

Now those same Mangala people were still camped down near Ngi Ngi or Mowla Bluff station. One day a bloke from the station by the name of Georgie Why came across them while he was out boundary riding, and he started demanding that they give him some scalps from their dingoes. An argument broke out and it ended with Georgie Why being knocked from his saddle with a boomerang and being speared through the leg. His horse took off back to the station and the manager there wondered what had happened. So he back-tracked the horse and found Georgie laying there with a spear through his leg. The manager took him back to the station and then sent a bloke up to Yeeda to ring the police.

Now those fellas who had speared Georgie Why thought the issue had been settled, and they just climbed up the hill and set up their camp. What they didn't know was that a party of police had been despatched from Derby with old Gunna Wyatpan and another Aboriginal bloke as their trackers. They headed straight down through Udialla and Sandfly, and crept up on those people during the night. When they had the camp surrounded they fired their guns and the people woke up to find the police standing over them.

The police got out their chains and locked all the people together; men, women, boys and girls. They had only come to arrest one person, the bloke who had speared Georgie Why, but Gunna told them that they should "clean the lot up". Well, that's what they decided to do.

First of all Gunna told them that the police were going to kill a bullock for dinner. He let them off the chain and told them to collect up a lot of firewood. When they had piled up enough, he told them that they would have to go back on the chain for a while and then they would all be released. The police boys did the chaining up because the police themselves were too wary to walk amongst a group of bush blackfellas. As soon as they were all on the chain again, the police got out their guns and started shooting them one by one.

They didn't ask any questions, they didn't have trials or anything of that sort, they didn't worry whether they were girls or boys, they just went ahead and killed them all. Some of them were shot; others, mainly the children, were whacked across the head.

Then they piled all the bodies up in a heap and burnt them. All because that one particular mongrel wanted revenge!

Only three people survived that massacre. One was an old man who had evaded capture at the camp. The other two were young women that the police saved for the manager at Mowla Bluff station. According to the old fella who told me the story there must have been three or four hundred people killed that day. It could have been more, it would be hard to tell. I'll have to go back there someday and have another look. Karpali Nyurtany used to be a camping place for those people, but after that the police took it over as one of their own camps.

I'll tell you another thing that used to happen in those days. If any of the station owners or managers wanted any of the young Aboriginal women, they considered it their privilege to take them. They used to clean them up and make them work around the homestead. If any coloured kids came along, they'd just tell those women to get rid of them. That did happen, and that's the truth. I know a lot of those old station managers were dirty old fellas because I've seen those things happen with my own eyes.

Titled: "Twenty Mile Sandy"

From my understanding of the judicial system, it would be too late now for Aboriginal people to take legal action over the things that were done to us. Even though we didn't have access to lawyers in those days, it's too late for us to do anything now. As far as claiming workers' compensation for injuries received on the stations, Aboriginal stockmen got nothing at all out of their injuries, yet there used to be a lot of accidents, people falling over with their horses, or getting thrown off, or getting kicked, broken arms, legs, or getting horned by a bullock.

We were excluded from receiving compo! Station owners and managers didn't seem too concerned either, if anyone got their bones broken. As long as the man could walk, he would be put onto plaiting ropes and making hobbles, or onto other jobs until his injury was better or his pain lessened. They still put them to work. I myself got thrown off a horse when I was about 11 years old and broke my collar bone. A neck injury still gives me trouble today. No compensation for the Aboriginal.

Now, I know the next door neighbours aren't any better than me. I can live side by side with white people; I can sit at the table and speak the same language. But at the same time, I must emphasise strongly that the Aboriginal culture, language and law is still practised today. People who say that our language and culture is finished are wrong. I still teach those things to my children. But for us the real problem comes when our children start going to school.

mberley, Johnine, Leila Watson.

Halls Creek, 1916.

I often wonder whether it's best for our kids to go to the kartiya schools or not. Today the kids get an education but they don't learn discipline. In our day education was more like apprenticeship. We all had our jobs to do and if we didn't do them we got a hiding. But they always explained the reason why we got the hiding. We were disciplined in a good way, and we knew who our bosses were. We learnt from both sides, the Aboriginal and the kartiya.

I have a feeling that it would be better if our kids were taught the way I was taught. That way they would get a better understanding of the kinship laws, the traditional laws which govern obligations, marriage, and all the social relations in our communities. The kartiya schools don't respect the skin group laws which, for instance, prohibit people from certain skin groups sitting close together, or even looking at each other. In the whiteman's schools, kids from those two skin groups are being put together. That's really breaking our culture down!

Fitzroy Crossing school, 1986.

Schools too often try to teach everything in the kartiya way. When those kids go home, their mothers might say to them in their own language, "Go and do that for me." Now, those kids are just as likely to turn around and answer back in English. In some places they don't even understand their parents' language and I think that's very sad.

Nowadays you see kids wandering around with their ear stuck to a tape recorder, or sitting with their eyes glued to the video. I think those things really undermine our culture, our heritage and our language. There's no give and take involved in those things; I'll tell you something that's really scarce: Aboriginal videos with Aboriginal stories in them being made for children.

I know that in the bigger communities the kids are getting outside the control of the parents. They go off with the bigger kids and start drinking and getting into trouble; they even start fighting with their parents. My parents were very strong. If I started answering back I got a clip over the ear! That's the sort of discipline I'd like to see brought back; but obviously I don't know whether it's going to happen. It's a very hard fight trying to educate our young people properly nowadays.

Fitzroy Crossing, main bridge.

Rosie Parks, fishing Brooking Channel of the Fitzroy in flood.

The bridge in the Wet.

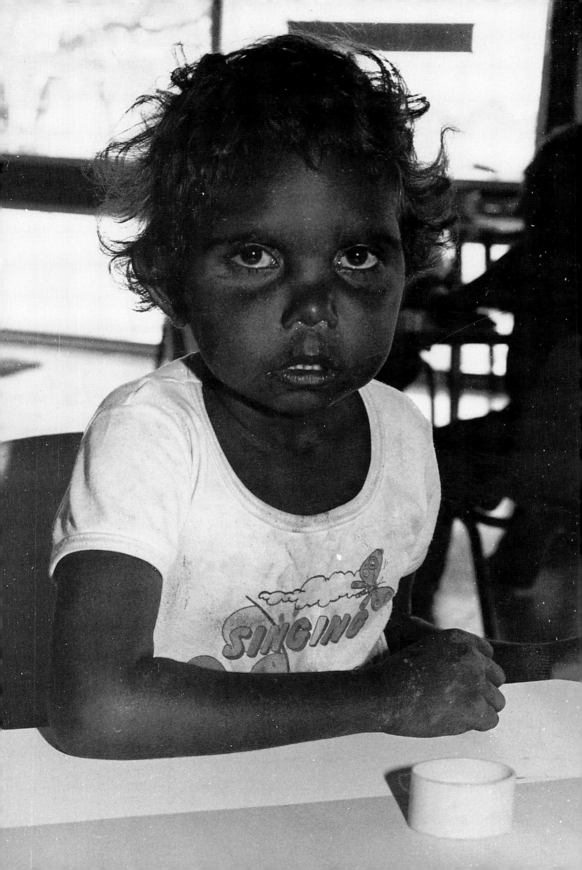

Two transfers in one year

This is how I left the station where I was brought up. Old Canny Rose bought a mule from Mt House and I broke him in because I had to ride him. That animal was jumping about, a madheaded mule - kick, strike and bite. Every time I got on him he used to bolt. He left me in the bush a couple of times and I had to walk back. So I gave the mule a flogging. That's what the old people told me to do in a case like that, flog him then walk him, so I gave him a flogging. Old Canny Rose heard about it and he went for me. "Don't belt that mule around, you've got to ride him all day."

Now all that year I'd been wanting to leave Mt Anderson several times. We were under the permit system. We couldn't leave without permission. That time I was man enough to walk off that place, and I joined my brother who was driving taxis in Derby. Then I went out to Camballin where I got a job checking water with surveyors. After a while they picked me out and put me in a job on better wages. I was made topman, on the pile driving tower.

The crane driver used to put me up by the hook. First they picked up a pile and dropped it into the sand, then they dropped the hammer on it, got it set harder, and when that was firm in the ground, I was put on top. I had to climb up the jib and they'd lower the jib with me on it and I'd take the shackle off the pile. I wasn't afraid of heights. Out on the stations I used to service the windmills. That meant climbing up on the platforms to change the oil, fix the gearbox, renew the cogs if they were worn. I was used to it.

There I was sitting on this one sheet of pile, 20 or 30 feet up. It was swinging about a bit and I started getting nervous. They put a step on the second one for me, welded it on, so I could stand on it while I was guiding the next one in, with someone down on the ground to help. That was all to stop the Fitzroy River running underneath the foundations of the dam, because it is all sand there. They couldn't do it without a man up there on top or the thing might just fall over.

ulie Yungubun, Fitzroy Crossing kindergarten (facing page).

Leopold Downs '86 sheet erosion.

Mt Anderson, 1987, surviving tussocks indicate the loss of topsoil.

opold Downs.

roded pasture downstream from the Camballin Barrage.

When I left they gave me a reference, and that's something I never got from the people I grew up with, out on the stations. I didn't even ask for it. They asked me, "Do you want a job?" and I said, "Yes." So they gave me a letter and sent me along to the Public Works Department in Derby, and they put me into a concreting gang. I did a lot of concreting work around Derby. Then I went over to Harbour and Lights, making pontoons, building the new jetty. So I had two transfers in one year.

They put in the first pile for the jetty, and some official fella in town hit the pile with a bottle of whisky and started the new jetty work. We built concrete pontoons for the crane barge, took them down to the water and floated them off. Some we built in the water and then pumped them out till they floated. When we had the barge made we put a big jib on it for a crane, to lift the pile. That was all built in the water while everything was floating. Then we added the steam hammer and started driving round piles and hexagonal piles, all of them very long on account of the 30 foot tides.

It was different, working nightshift too, according to the tide, not like on the stations. You couldn't sit down and have a smoke, you could stand around but you couldn't sit down. And the pay was much better than on the stations too. We had to work for it though, we couldn't carry another man. If you did your job you were all right, the foreman wouldn't say anything. If you didn't, he'd come for you. Gunsmoke, my brother called him. He was on to you but he was fair, just wouldn't put up with any humbug.

"You better come over and collect your pay," this fella said. So I did, I signed for it and they gave me a packet with all these notes in it and I counted them up. Now on the station we were getting maybe five pound a month clear, but there was more money in that pay packet than you'd make in a year on the station. I just counted the notes over and couldn't believe it, more than 200 pounds.

It surprised me, you know. I thought, what's all this money doing here? I walked away and talked to my brother, and he had the same. The following pay was even better. I counted it, hundreds of pounds.

Well, I didn't have much clothing you know, coming in from the station, so I got everything I needed, some nice fancy cowboy shirts, boots, hat and so on. It didn't take much money. And the second pay I bought a motorcar, a Prefect, so I had wheels. Then after 12 months they paid my fare to Darwin, where my sister lived, for a holiday. That's more than the station ever did. On stations people got rations and went down to the river for holidays.

I left Harbour and Lights like this. My mate worked on the motorboat, jumping around from pile to pile. He was on the planks over the water and he couldn't swim a stroke. But he was a good worker. Then one day they sacked him, I don't know why. The union had a big meeting about it. They didn't involve us, we just went on working. They went to some court over it and he was reinstated. But he came to me and said, "Now they're going to be looking over my shoulder, and yours too, watching everything, so I think I'll go." And we both went, though it was a big comedown in pay going back on the stations.

"I'm taking those two little horses."

I went to Nerrima because I knew that work. They were paying better and I was on 20 pound a month. But I really fell out with the new manager there, Joe D. It was when we were doing a tandem muster, that's two stations combining. We had 14 or 15 stockmen, Kalyeeda had only four or five, not enough to tail or muster, so we'd give them a hand. You call that tandem mustering.

We used to send away about thirteen hundred cattle from Nerrima, so we had to replace the bullocks we sent off. We'd do that with young cattle from Jubilee, which was the breeding ground. Cassie Torres brought a mob of weaners down from there, that's what you call steers before they become bullocks. I took over responsibility for the waybills and other things, got the mob off him and put them into our paddock, ready for branding. Before we branded them we had a drink of tea and something. By then we had managed to get four or five trucks of the bullocks away.

239

One thing you had to do was divide up the cattle. They'd get mixed up from the stations. So you'd bring them all together and the managers of the four stations would be there too, Nerrima, Kalyeeda, Millijidee, Noonkanbah. They'd have a meeting and talk about it while you were doing it.

You cut them out, although you can't see out in the herd, for the dust and there's too many for a close look. Sometimes we used to put them through the yard, one for you, one for you, one for you. We marked down who they were for. Or if the managers were happy with it, you said, "All right, give us 12 bulls or whatever, that'll settle it, you can have the rest." We'd say, "I'll catch you next time." That's how we used to work.

I don't know why but this time the managers were all in dispute. They were short of bullocks, that might have been the problem. Normally they are never there, while you're working. The previous managers had kept pretty quiet when they did come out. Anyhow, they were having a row amongst themselves when I came back to the camp after getting the other mob into the yard.

Rugby Yard, mustered for the trucks.

This manager Joe wanted to balance his trucks, so I gave him two or three hundred. They divide them up but it's all the same company owning all the stations, all the same money!

Then Joe came over to me and said, "Look, I've worked on these places before, I want to see the place running better." I said, "Oh yeah, that's all right, but at this moment you know, you can't sort of put me off doing what I'm doing."

This job was normal practice, you know, it was everyday. If you want to change anything you sit down and talk somewhere about what changes you want, not on the job. Otherwise we'd be in for it. Now what we were doing was educating the wild cattle. That is one important thing, because any wild cattle will bust a yard up for you and so they've got to be quietened down before it's time to ship them. So you run them with the others for a while till they get educated. We took off with this mob of bullocks from there to a place called Karlu Karlu, in the top part of Broken Wagon.

I left Cassie with one mob and I was taking off with my lot for Nerrima, when Joe D followed me and said, "I've got to know what you're doing." I said, "Stuff it, you do know, you're the manager."

Joe D had just come up with our swags, brought up the swags, that's all, when he saw me riding around with this mob. He said, "But I've got to know what you're doing." I said, "Well, we're taking this mob across there." "Do you know what to do with them?" he said. I was fed up. "Of course, we're going across the other side. I want to give them a spell. This is my job, it's not the first time I'm taking a mob. I've been told before what to do with cattle."

It is the usual thing after walking them all that way and they've come across the river. At maybe eight, nine o'clock, you settle them down and feed them all day. Then they're full, contented and that night you watch them. In the morning when you start, you can split them in two mobs, take them one way, drop them off, you've got to mix the mob up, take them slowly, don't stir them up. You mix them, because if you don't some cattle will take off the way they came from. They'll get lost, caught in the corner of a fence, and they can perish somewhere. So we used to do that, spell them out, then mix them.

Old Mac, the manager from Jubilee, came over and asked me, "I hear Joe's having a bit of a dispute with you." I said, "No, my job is cattle work, his job is manager. He's the paperwork, you know? I never had trouble last year or the year before and I don't know about these changes. We always sat down and talked about what we going to do, how many cattle to send off, what horses to brand, how many horses we cut - we have discussions, you know?" "Yes," he says, "right. Well if you don't want to work here, you can come over to Jubilee." I said, "If I go, then I'm taking those two little horses. "

See they bloody near shot these two horses. They were sort of wild, you know. You have to treat a horse in its kind. Mac went up to Joe and said, "He'll want to take them horses." But Joe said, "He doesn't own them, he can't take them." Now Mac was from the same company and he offered to send back another three, but Joe D wouldn't have it. "He can't take 'em."

Well that was that. I went up to Jubilee and started working. And then Ted McLarty came round. He was the owner of the whole thing. Well he had shares in the company, put it that way. Word got around to old Ted and he told one of his men, "Look, take Johnny's horses, take them, and swap them over." So I got them back.

Those horses had been pretty wild when we'd broken them in. One of them jumped over the rail and ripped his guts open. I had to knock him down and stitch him up right there and then. This happened on Nerrima and old Ted was there. He was there while I was doing it, and he said, "Ah - you should shoot him." But I stitched him up because he was my horse. And Ted said when he saw this, "You can have the bloody thing, if you spend that much time with him!" He gave me that horse, but Joe wouldn't let me have him.

With our young fellas we're not trying to overrule them. We don't say, "You're in my gang, you stay in my gang." We try to show them how you can flow in relationship. If we're not doing enough here, we've got to go over there and give them a hand, sort of bog in. We want to build that relationship to try and work all round the station. We had that experience.

You see, once you're on your job, away you go, because you know it. That might be spaying or branding. I learnt all that, by just being there, I helped in the crush, and saw them spaying a few times. Then as a young fella you are given your head, you watch it and then you do it, they give you the knife, they make a cut and give you the knife, and in you go. I learnt that from Chum Lee and he was the quickest of them all, two minutes and he had the cow sewn up real neat. Some of them would leave a big lump, and there'd be a sore. You'd know for a long time that cow had been spayed, but not with those Chum Lee did. We'd have to cut the ear to show it had been done. We'd spay the ones we didn't want to breed because they might be a breed we didn't want, like a strawberry roan.

I'll tell you about another manager that I had there. I stayed on at Jubilee working with old MacNamara. My job was head stockman and he let me get on with it, because I knew the work. Then old Mac got sick; it was cancer, very sad. They took him into Derby Hospital and his wife stayed on Jubilee a while. Then she went on to join him, and I was left in charge. I asked McLarty what he wanted me to do and he said, "You stay, go on doing your job."

They got in a new manager, a sheep farmer from down south, but it's a different situation in this country; we were running cattle through the scrub, not in cleared and fenced paddocks where you could see everything. He had us running around doing all these little jobs that he could think of. Now on a station everyone knows what needs to be done. If you're head stockman you have your jobs, you don't have to be told. And you don't tell your gang what to do all the time, only when something's not going as it should.

Anyway, the Christmas holidays came along and we packed up, greased the saddles and gear and put it all away. We were about to take our work horses out and let them go bush for their feed, when this new manager came along. He took me and the men off that and had us running around doing what he wanted. Well, when Christmas comes you can't shift it. So off I went for a fortnight's holiday.

When I came back the horses were still there, and they were thin. I went up and said to this farmer manager bloke, "What's this? These are our work horses, they're on poor tucker, still in the station paddock!" They were all bones you know, nothing to eat. And he said, "That's your job." He put it on me.

So I opened the gate for the horses and took them out. Rode with them down to a good place about 18 k's from the station, where there was plenty of water and feed. I took them out real slow, because you have to be careful, they're weak. I and another bloke. And that manager, he knew I was taking them out. And we let them go, took our saddles off the two we rode and let them go with the rest.

We waited there. No-one came for us. So we carried our saddles under a tree. And we're wondering if they got bogged coming for us. You never leave anyone out like that on the stations, if you know where they are, you go out and get them, or if you don't know, you look for them. We just expected them to be coming out to collect us with a vehicle, but they didn't come.

So we walked back the 18 k's following down the road. We expected to see them coming for us. But we got all the way back. So I went to see this manager and I said, "Look, I can't work like this." And he said, "All right, you can go."

Ambrose Phillips, Gibb River Station.

I couldn't work with him. Not only myself but the windmill man too was having the same trouble, and he was good. I saw him build a boring plant over the wet at Nerrima. He made up the roller, the winch drum for the cable, the hoist, put in the motor, everything. He could weld aluminium - first time I ever saw that done. And this windmill man, he said, "Well, I'm going too."

It was a blow up, by management. Now the usual practice is for them to take you somewhere, drop you off in town, 'cos you can't stay on the station. But this fella didn't, he wouldn't. We were supposed to walk the 30 kms from Jubilee to Fitzroy Crossing. Then the rest of the young fellas there said, "All right, we're going too." That's how I got out, we had a car between us. The manager said, "I'll get your money," but he didn't pay the full amount. In town I got on to McLarty's and they fixed it up.

A married man and a wanted man

Now a third manager was on Nerrima, a married man and a wanted man, but we didn't know that at the time. He was from the east, Victoria, and we were mustering. We had an order for 700 cattle. Only way to catch them was to close the water off and to moonlight them. So we went out to Big Flow. This manager, Greg, came to where we had some horses ready for the drafting and he said, "Which is the boss's horse?" Now these were camp horses, they were trained that way, they didn't know anything else, they weren't for mustering. Well, so they pointed one of them out to him, the best camp horse there, for drafting. But they couldn't tell him that, he was the manager. And he saddled it up and came out with us, and we could see it was a camp horse he was on.

And off he goes, this manager, but the horse under him must have known something was wrong; this wasn't drafting, and they're smart you know. Anyway it bucked around a bit and threw him. And then it galloped off. So one of the fellas collected it, but he didn't take it back to the manager, he wanted to show him something, so he took it back to the camp. The manager had to walk back to Big Flow.

Benjamin Desert (Heathcliffe), Noonkanbah rodeo 1986.

He didn't say anything when we'd camped the cattle and came in for the night. He must have been storing it up. A couple of days later he got on the same horse again, and out he came to join us. He was telling me do this, do that, so I said to him, "Look, don't tell me my job, you've got yours and I've got mine. And that goes for these men out here - I'll tell them what to do, if they need it."

That afternoon we went out and there was a big mob, seven or eight hundred cattle, we saw them at Green Spring, and they took off. That's when you don't need to tell people, they know their job, they see the cattle go and bang, they're off too. After we had rounded them up, I went up to Greg and I said, "What about this lot of cattle, bring 'em together?" That's when he told me, "No, far as I'm concerned you buggers are sacked." "Right here?" I asked him. And he said, "Yes, right here, you're sacked." So I turned my horse and went back to the camp.

When the rest of the men saw me riding off, they came too, because they thought of me as the man they worked with, so he sacked the lot. Back in the camp we talked amongst ourselves and

246

the story was sorted out. Then he said that he had changed his mind, and that he was going to keep me on. I didn't stay because he still wanted to sack the rest. We went back to the station and he paid them. Now some of those fellas had three or four month's wages owing to them, and they weren't getting the right dollar, he was telling them they'd been booking this up, booking that up.

The next morning I was having a shower when the police arrived. There was a knock on the door and I said, "I'm in the bath, who is it?" They didn't say they were the police. When I opened the door a uniform was looking at me. I didn't have any clothes on, just a towel round me. "I want you to help me," the sergeant said, "I've got to arrest your manager." I said, "Oh yeah?" I didn't ask any more questions.

They wanted me to go in there and get all the rifles. So I dressed and went up to the house with Malachi Smith. While I was talking to this Greg fella, Malachi looked through the house, found the station rifles and sneaked off with them. Then he told the sergeant it was all clear. When the police walked in this Greg fella shattered a bit. They gave him the warrant, grabbed him, turned him around and threw the handcuffs on him. I don't know what he had done. It must have been more than take a car for them to tie his hands behind his back.

The police said to me, "You can't leave those cattle out there." I said, "I've been sacked." The cattle were still there, quite a mob, about a thousand. We had a waybill for them and the trucks were coming. So we got them that night and put them in the yard. Then we went out early in the morning before light, and planted our stockmen all round the yard.

When those cattle see where they are, some of them jump over the rails. You can't take them straight back in, you pull them down and tie their legs, until they quieten down together and you've got a little mob, then you take them back in.

The owners came there that night too. They were interested in the cattle but they were more worried about their workers walking off. They were good bosses, McLartys, always worried about their workers getting enough tucker, that kind of thing.

Shot out for nothing

A lot of the people being put in charge of the stations nowadays don't know anything about the environment up here. They call themselves managers, but they haven't stopped to learn from the old managers or from people like myself, people who've lived up here for a long time. It's important to know the right time to burn the country and the right places to burn. Otherwise a lot of damage can be done to the natural environment. You see, by burning the country the right way you're actually cultivating the land so that particular bush foods will flourish; you're encouraging animals to come into the area to breed.

Today, some of those so-called station managers are burning at the wrong time, and they're burning the wrong places. They're killing off a lot of wildlife by doing that and they're knocking back a lot of the native fruit trees. They're really only interested in getting green pick for their cattle. They either don't know, or don't care, about all the birds who have young in their nests. I'd like to see all that change. The Aboriginal people have an intimate understanding of the natural environment, but we haven't been given the opportunity to apply that knowledge in modern jobs. I think the Government should give us the chance to be involved in the management of our country.

You know, when I was young you could drive down the road and you'd see kangaroos, turkeys, emus and all sorts of bush animals. Today there are very few of those things left. In the old days people used to walk from Noonkanbah to Mt Anderson, and they'd have no worries at all about finding enough food along the track to keep them going. But you'd have no hope of doing that today.

A lot of those things, such as the kangaroos and emus, were shot out for nothing. They cut the kangaroo right down because they said it was a pest. Actually, it was one of the real cultivators. Even though they were digging up the roots of the grass to eat, kangaroos were making holes which grass seeds would wash into. They actually helped to cultivate those grasses. Now the roos have almost gone from this country. The sheep and cattle took their place and they overgrazed the whole Fitzroy River frontage.

People who have been around in this country for a long while can point out the way the clumps of grass are sitting higher than the surrounding ground. The only thing holding that bit of soil in place is that clump of grass; where it has its roots the soil hasn't washed away but the rest of the surrounding topsoil has. In some areas it has eroded right down to the hard soil underneath, and no grass will grow there any more. Years ago the grass used to grow very well in those places, and the topsoil used to be soft and deep.

When the sheep and cattle used to walk through those areas, they used to wear a groove into the topsoil. Seeds used to fall or blow into that groove, and when the wet came it would wash into there too, and those seeds would grow. Nowadays, when cattle walk through there they don't even leave a track. Any seeds falling onto that ground now are just blown away by the wind.

The pastoral industry built all the stations in the Kimberley, including those along the Fitzroy River. Nonetheless, the cattle and sheep have done a lot of damage to this country. Aboriginal people provided the workforce for the stations but they never had a say on what was happening to their country. The same thing can be said about the Camballin dam. Aboriginal people were never consulted, the Government just went ahead and built it. It was purely a question of economics. I helped build the thing in 1959 and I got a few thousand dollars out of it. When I look at it now I can see what wrong I've done. At the time I didn't know that I was doing such great damage to my country.

The dam brought a lot of erosion to the river but recently they constructed an all-weather road across the Fitzroy flood plain and that did even more damage. I first noticed the erosion when the Broome road was just a low track, before they even built what my brother calls the China Wall. The water started cutting dirt and making channels across the flood plains. That's because it wasn't flowing through in the natural way.

I was young when they first put that road in and I thought it was a good thing. I used to like travelling across to Broome to see all the pretty girls there. As I got a bit older, I started to realise that those flood plains were being ruined. But that was nothing compared to the damage the new road has caused. Whoever designed it didn't know this country. That road banked up the floodwaters right back from Willare to Fitzroy Crossing, hundreds of kilometres of river. The water covered areas I've never seen flooded before, even in a big flood. It ran through areas I've never seen it run through before.

When I was a kid the main channel used to be quite narrow, but now look at it. We used to be able to swim across when it was in flood, even though it used to be a mile or a mile and a half wide. We used to swim across to one island, then to another island, then reach that other side. Nowadays you couldn't do that because you wouldn't even be able to see those islands. The river runs about five miles wide, in flood, and it's unbroken water from one side to the other. If you were going to swim it, you'd have to swim all the way. And that's how much it has changed since the 'fifties. There's a flood-line up in the trees, from the mud and rubbish, and I could tell from it that those river islands had been covered by 10 or 11 feet of water during the '86 flood. There wouldn't have been much of an island for the trapped cattle, or anything else, to survive on.

At the height of that flood, ABC radio carried a news report about a mob of cattle that had been washed down the river. They were supposed to have landed at the Derby jetty, climbed up the boat ramp and walked back to Yeeda. It was a big joke to some people, but it sounded like a lot of bull to me. There may have been a few cattle that survived and managed to climb ashore at Derby, but a lot were drowned between Lanji and Yeeda, and horses with them.

That stock should have been mustered before the floodwaters rose. We would never leave our stock where they might drown, if we thought there might be a big flood. And if we knew those animals were on the frontage we used to try and help them get out before the channels really filled up. You'd have to be a pretty cruel sort of a fella if you didn't.

I went down the old track from Yeeda to Lanji Crossing about six months after the flood and I came across the carcasses of about 17 or 18 horses laying on the island there. Now from what the old people have told me, that island never used to go under water, even in a big flood. It obviously did go under that time. This must have happened when the Main Roads blasted a section of the China Wall to release some of the pressure. I guess they were trying to minimise the damage to their newly completed $8.9 million section of the road. When that section of the wall was blown and the water started rushing through, it sucked the backwater out of all the waterholes upstream. Just as if somebody had put a hose in them and siphoned them dry.

Not only that, the sudden release of water scoured a lot of our country. It caused big washaways along the bank of the creek which runs past Mt Anderson homestead. The road from Mt Anderson to the Looma turnoff has always been an all-weather road, except for a few little creek crossings. Depending on how much rain falls in the hills there, you only have to wait for half an hour or an hour before you can drive across them. But during the '86 flood those creeks really filled up; and when they dynamited at Willare, the rushing water just cut our creek banks to pieces.

oured creek, Mt Anderson station.

Janet Williams with kindegarten children, Fitzroy riverbed at low water level.

Israeli people have bought Camballin now, and they're thinking about building another dam. Not on the Fitzroy River itself, but a dam to catch the water coming off several creeks that feed the Fitzroy. They want to expand their irrigation further north towards the highway. Those are good flats, good growing country. But if that new dam goes ahead it's going to damage Aboriginal interests in the area. The people from Looma used to go hunting there all year round, and especially during the dry season. During the wet we would mainly hunt in the high country. Now they're planning to farm all our good hunting areas! For a while now we've found it difficult to get access to those places because the owners, both past and present, have been locking the gates. Aboriginal people used to go out fishing along the Seventeen Mile Dam but they've been chased away from there by the Camballin mob and a lot of them are scared to go back.

There's a cave at Mt Anderson that has a lot of history attached to it. When we get a chance we'd like to fence it off from the cattle and turn it into a wildlife sanctuary. The old manager used to call it the "Pindan Ram Paddock Cave" but its proper name is Lina Nyurtany. It's down near the western end of Jarlmadanga, the hill that the kartiyas call Mt Anderson. There's a permanent waterhole in that cave, fed by a spring that trickles out of a fissure in the rock. It also has an opening in the roof, and years ago a giant fig tree grew from that pool right up through that opening. Its roots used to reach right down from the lip of that opening to the pool of water below. It was possible to climb up that tree, over the lip, and onto the ridge top.

Our people used to hide out up there if the police were after them; and they used to climb down to the pool and fill up their water containers. They would sit up the top there and watch the police come into the cave looking for tracks. But, of course, those people were careful not to leave any tracks. They didn't need to come down to the lowlands to hunt because there was plenty of tucker up on those hills, such as kangaroos, porcupines, and snakes. When the police had left the station some of the people from the camp would go up and pass the word on. So those people would be able to come down again.

That old fig tree is gone now but some of its roots are still there. There are paintings on the walls of that cave too, and they used to have significance when I was a kid. They used to be beautiful paintings. But the mud-larks and wasps have made their nests on the walls and some of the paintings have been spoilt. Because the bore outside is broken down, the cattle have been going into the cave for a drink and they've messed the place up too.

The responsibility for caring for that cave and its paintings has fallen on us now, since we're the only people left. Most of our old people are gone, and the ones who are left are too weak to get up and do those sort of things. But we haven't had a chance! The station was only bought for the Aboriginal people three years ago, and we're still cleaning up the mess that was left behind. We haven't had a chance to do our own thing yet.

CHAPTER 9

You can go back to your place if you want to

Barney Barnes

Walmajarri man (Born 1918? -)

Nyipayarri (Bush name)   Jangkarti (Skin name)

I wasn't sure I liked the station life

I was born out in the desert. I remember when I was a little kid, my father used to take me on walkabout all around the desert; you know, walking around in the bush. We used to eat all the different types of meat: barni (that's goanna), snake, porcupine, kangaroo, wallaby, everything. We even ate grass seeds. You grind them up with a stone and make a sort of a flour. Then you mix that with water until you get something like a pudding, which you then bake. We used to put it in some bark from a tree, chuck it on the coals, cover it up with some more bark, and scrape some hot coals on top of it. When it's baked, it's just like a bread. That's what we'd eat with the dry meat and dry fruit.

My father hunted with a spear; he speared all those animals I named. The women went around with their coolamons and collected the grass seeds and fruit. They'd grind the seeds with a stone and cook them in the fire. We had no plates. We didn't have blankets either. We used to sleep on the ground with a fire on each side, one at our feet and one at our heads. It gets cold out in the desert you know. In the cold weather, we'd have to pile up some grass to make a windbreak. But during the summer months, we'd just have a little fire to keep the mosquitos down. We wouldn't camp where there were a lot of mosquitos, because they'd bite us everywhere, since we had nothing on. All we could do was to have a smoky fire going all night.

When we wake up in the morning, the only thing we have for breakfast would be the leftover meat and sugarbag. That's all. But there was plenty of sugarbag and plenty of kangaroos, that big red bush kangaroo, not the river kangaroo. We ate all kinds of meat, including blue-tongue lizards and snakes. But there are not many snakes or kangaroos around nowadays.

Sometimes when they couldn't find any kangaroos, some blackfellas would go and find a bullock to kill; they'd steal one from the kartiya. I didn't know what they were doing, I was just a kid. They just gave me a feed. But the station manager came up and saw the tracks of cattle galloping everywhere, and he wrote a letter down to the police station calling on them to go out after those blackfellas.

Broome police with the Chief Inspector on inland patrol. 1940s.

One morning the police came out and found our mob. They got their chain and put it around the people's necks. I don't know how many blackfellas they chained up, but it was too many.

soners from Stuart's Creek 400 miles inland on their way down, 9 miles from Wyndham, 22.8.06.

They chained up women and children too! All the people were taken down to the police station and put on trial. My father didn't know anything about the cattle killing business. He told them, "I've never killed any bullocks, some other people did that. I never did anything wrong." So they sent him to Christmas Creek and he had to work there.

Mobs of our people were sent to Christmas Creek. That manager made the police go out and bring all the people in from the desert. He reckoned that they were killing too many bullocks. So the police came out and rounded up all the Walmajarri people. It's Walmajarri country all around there, around Christmas Creek, right through to Kalyeeda, down the Canning Stock Route, and right through to Billiluna. All that area is Walmajarri. It seemed like there were millions of people in the desert in those early days but it's all changed now.

The police came and took everybody away to the stations, the whole people. The Halls Creek police worked the eastern side, the Fitzroy police worked this side, and the Broome police worked the western side. They kept going at it until nobody was left out there. They didn't allow the Aboriginal people to live in the desert after that. They sent some of the people to Cherrabun, some to Go Go, and some to Christmas Creek. They put all the Walmajarri people into the stations, and worked them hard.

Moola Bulla station, 1910-18.

Violet Valley station stores unloading, 1910-18.

They had to work on the stations all year round, though they let people go to ceremonies during the wet. Sometimes the ceremonies would be at Bohemia Downs or Go Go, and sometimes at Christmas Creek. No-one was left behind in the desert.

We were doing a lot of jobs at the station and we didn't have a chance to worry about all those places anymore. But one day a lot of people ran away in the middle of the night and went back to their country again, and I went with them. I was just a kid then. We were happy out in the desert. A lot of people, all gone out into the bush south of Christmas Creek.

The manager found out that we had taken off and the next day he sent for the police. The police went out and rounded up all the people again; nobody escaped. We were all brought back to the station. There was a lot of cattle running this side of the desert; but there weren't any in the desert itself. Cattle were all over the Emanuel block, running all over the pastoral lease area. But the desert had nothing to do with that. Our country was more on the desert side.

But still the police went right through there and rounded up all the people. That was the last time we ran away; we didn't try to go back to the desert again after that. Some of the old people were allowed to stay out there; but they started dying. There was a lot of disease for which we didn't have any medicine. The manager had all the young people working and there would have only been two or three old people living on the station by that time.

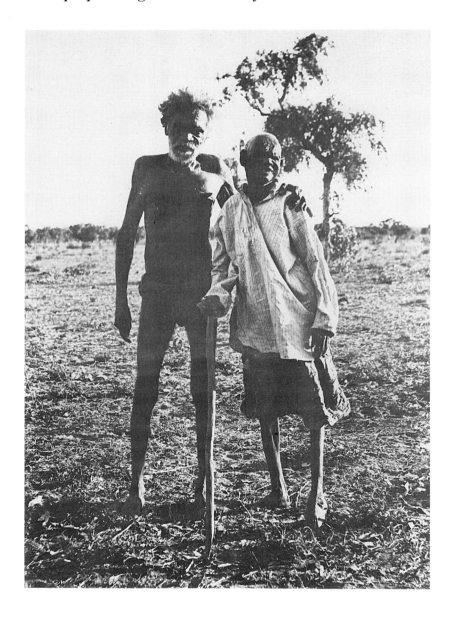

Station workers, north-west early 20th C.

They gave me a job, and I started doing a lot of work for the whiteman. Us blackfellas did all sorts of work. We kept thinking about the desert, but there was no-one left out there. From Christmas Creek right down into the desert, there was nobody left in all that country except some old people.

I worked on Christmas Creek for years. When the wet came they'd let us go on holidays, though they'd keep a few fellas working. They'd often be the people who were being punished, blokes who had run away from the station. Nobody would know where they had gone, so the manager would go and tell the police. If the police found that bloke, they put a chain around his neck and take him back to the station.

Or maybe they'd send him to jail in Broome and put him to work around there. Some people were even sent on ships to Fremantle I think. When they let them go, they'd have to walk back to their home; walk back to Christmas Creek or wherever. No ride in a motorcar! They just let them go in Broome and told them to walk back. I don't know how many people that happened to, but it was too many. Some of them died along the way I think. Others made it back to the station and their families, so the manager would put them back to work.

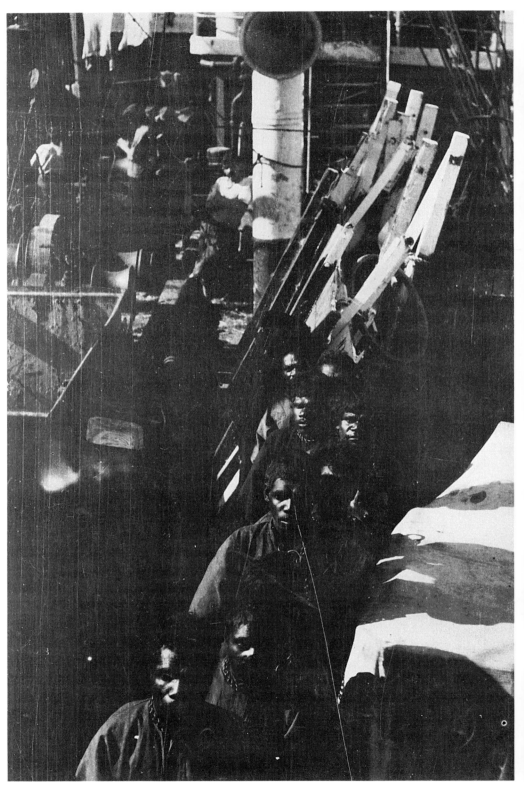

Kimberley prisoners going south by steamer early 20th C.

Before we went to the stations we had never eaten kartiya bread or drunk tea; we didn't know about those things. I liked the taste of kartiya food, it was very good. But some of the people were unsure about it. I wasn't sure I liked the station life. I was thinking about the bush life all the time. But kartiya were giving me tea to drink, and cake or a bit of fruit. They'd give us porridge every morning with some milk. It was cow milk, not nannygoat milk. We didn't have any nannygoats then. They gave me hot milk every morning. The cook was a kartiya. He used to separate the milk with help from two or three Aboriginal women. We had it easy at first.

Violet Valley station.

Then we came into disease, and the old people started to die, until there was none left. The new generation, all the young people, were working on the station. There was nothing left of the old generation. There aren't many people alive now who were born out in the desert. A lot of young people were born on Christmas Creek and belong to the station country. My wife and I would be the only desert Walmajarri left in Derby. I don't know how many would be in Fitzroy Crossing. Just a handful. A lot of the people who are on Christmas Creek now are from a different mob; they're Wangkatjunga people from the other side of our country.

Early station establishment.

There weren't many kartiya on the station in those days; just the cook, the manager, a station hand, and the head stockman. That's all, four. Not many. And there were no kartiya women. They came along later. One bloke who came to manage the station in the more recent times had a missus. That was Arthur Millard. He brought his kartiya wife up. Before that, white women had never come here, because the country was too hard for them.

Halls Creek, 1918.

All the work on the station was done by the Aborigine. There was one kartiya working man who would keep all the old people on the job, and the head stockman would be with the cattle. Then there was the manager and the cook. The cook would bake bread and cook everything for the station, and he'd keep all the women working. The women used to clean the homestead; they'd clean everything. They had to pick up all the paper and rubbish and chuck it on the rubbish pile. They would even sweep right around the house to get rid of the dust, or something like that. Some of the women worked in the kitchen. There was a big stove in the kitchen, and the cook would have all those women making bread and cooking meat. He kept them all working.

There was no bore at the homestead, so all the water had to be carried up to the homestead by bucket. That was done by the women too. I don't know how far it was down to the river at Christmas Creek, but it must have seemed like miles to the women carrying those buckets. I couldn't say how many women they had doing that job, it might have been a hundred. They carried the buckets up on their heads in the blackfella way, not across the shoulders in the Chinese way. They would go down to the river, get a bucket of water, carry it back to the station, and pour it into the tanks. They had very big tanks there. Bigger than any you'd see in Derby. They were big, silver, ready-made ones, and there might have been three or four of them.

After breakfast, at about eight o'clock, the women would go down to the creek and fill up their buckets. Both young women and old. They would leave a couple of old women at the camp to look after all the children. They carried bucketful after bucketful of water on their heads up to those tanks. They'd knock off at eleven o'clock. In those days they only worked in the morning, not in the afternoon.

The station didn't have a motorcar back then, though we did have one bullock wagon. After a while they got a donkey cart with a big tray, and an old bloke to drive it. They'd put all the buckets on there and take them down to the river. It made it much easier for those women. They just filled the buckets up and the wagon carried the water back to the homestead. But it was very hard for the women in the days when the homestead had no water. It was hard work carrying those buckets. Sometimes everyone who wasn't working on another job would be down at the river helping the women fill those buckets.

Moola Bulla stockmen and boy, 1920s.

I lived in the Aboriginal camp on the station with my mother and father, but when I was about 8 years old my father died. Another father, Jinayikan (old Billy Barnes) adopted me; he married my mother Yakulu (Angelina) and grew me up. That father started me working in the cattle jobs. I helped him on whatever he was doing, which was mainly yard-building. I was still a young boy at the time. When I got a bit older, the manager started working me; started giving me jobs to do. Then, when I got to be about 13 or 14 years old, the manager put me onto a horse and I started doing mustering and all that sort of work.

Noonkanbah, 1940s.

It was a rough time for us in those days. They had all the Aboriginal people working hard, and they even made the old people work. But they didn't give those old people anything, not even clothes. They started making us work in the afternoon too. That was just for our tucker, and for some of us a bit of clothing, working clothes. The managers and the other white workers gave the Aboriginal people a lot of flack. One manager at Christmas Creek, Vic Jones, was all right, but some of those other white blokes were too rough. They even used to give hidings to old people and young people, and kick them with their boots to make them work harder.

Moola Bulla killer, station distribution, 1920s.

Everything will be good now

One day when I was about 13 years old we had some trouble on the station. The manager Bert Smith had been fighting with an Aboriginal boy, and he sang out for a rifle. So, the kartiya cook came along and shot that young bloke. Shot him! He was a good young boy; I don't know why they did that. He didn't do anything wrong. There were a lot of people there at the time who saw it happen. Women and children, everybody was there. Right, then they got wood from the woodheap and some kerosene. They chucked that boy on top and lit the fire up. They didn't bury him in a grave, they just chucked him on the fire. Everybody was watching, but they couldn't do anything. Some of them started crying but the manager pointed the gun at them and told them, "Shut up before I blow you buggers out!" Some of the fellas started grumbling amongst themselves, but the manager went at them with his gun and made them go back to work.

In those days, we really worried for people, because the whiteman had done a lot of things like that. All the people were frightened. But it started to get a bit easier in 1944. That's when the Government sent us help. A doctor came and looked at all the people, to check for leprosy and to attend to those who were sick. And he brought a lot of nurses with him. It made it easier for us then, we got medicine for the sick people, and we started having plenty of fruit.

I think that doctor's name was Dr Musso. (District Medical Officer, Fitzroy Crossing 1940s - Ed.) He went all round the country and told the Aboriginal people, "We're going to make it a lot easier for you people. This is your country, your place." Dr Musso came and told them that. He went and saw the owners and told them to make it easier for the blackfellas, told them to give us plenty of fruit, clothes and everything. It started to get easier for us from that time on.

Before that we had a real rough time. There was no government looking out for us. Nothing! Then the doctor came and said, "Everything will be good now. Aboriginal people are going to get medicine right across the nation. We'll gather up all the sick children, take them into Derby Hospital, give them medicine and cure them up." Before then, those kids got nothing; they just used to die. Although sometimes someone used to help them. Men and women would lie in the camp sick until they died. They never got anything, no medicine and no help at all. A rough time in those early days. Then the doctor started coming, and he said everything would be all right.

There was no school at Christmas Creek when I was a kid, so the manager used to put us to work. But the station didn't give working clothes to the kids. We were riding horses in short pants, not long trousers, and we didn't have boots or hats.

If some kid slept in, the others used to chuck some water under his blanket to make him get up. Otherwise he might have got a flogging from the manager. The manager even used to flog kids with a whip sometimes.

When I was young, my father took me everywhere droving horses. We even drove a thousand head of horses once. We used to get a lot of horses from Anna Plains, Pardoo and De Grey stations. We'd go down to there from Christmas Creek, pick up a mob of horses and drove them all the way back to Christmas Creek. Just four people, me, my old man, an old whiteman and a young whiteman. I was just a boy at the time.

Horses are a lot harder to drove than cattle, and more dangerous. Cattle are much quieter. It's hard to stop horses taking off during the night. They'd be walking all over the plain, trying to get away back to their country.

We had to watch them all the way because in a lot of places there were no yards. We used to take them right up through old Bidyadanga. Not that new place where the La Grange Mission is now. I've never been to there. There were no Aboriginal people at Bidyadanga in those days, it was just a post office. There were a few Aboriginal people at Thangoo, but they were from a different mob, they were coastal people.

We took those horses right up through Thangoo station and up to Roebuck Plains, then drove them through to Nilapaplikan and on towards Yeeda. I remember one trip when all the creeks were in flood and we had to cross the Fitzroy River at Cockatoo Yard. That's a dry island in the middle of the river there and we had to swim 600 horses across. That was hard going, by jingo!

Noonkanbah, 1915.

Jimbo Johnson, Mt Barnett.

We took them to Yeeda and stopped there for a week to have a spell. From Yeeda we took them down to Lower Liveringa and then through Mt Anderson, Upper Liveringa and Noonkanbah.

We had a camp for a little while at Noonkanbah, and then took them on to Christmas Creek. We didn't lose any of those horses. By the time we got them to Christmas Creek they had got to know us, and had settled down.

The next year we went to Argyle station, picked up 200 horses and brought them back to Christmas Creek. Just two whitemen, my father, me and my cousin, Kylie Nixon. Argyle was a station back then, though it's just a dam today. I did a lot of work with my old man. After that, we started droving bullocks. We used to pick up 500 bullocks at a time from the bullock paddock on Christmas Creek, and drove them right through to Derby for loading onto the ship.

I've done a lot of droving in my time, from Christmas Creek, Go Go, Cherrabun, Jubilee Downs, Brooking Springs and Fossil Downs. First off, I was doing contract droving with an old kartiya bloke called Billy Cox. We used to call him "Billygoat." After he died, we started working for a half-caste bloke from Marble Bar by the name of Clancy Doggety. And after that I was droving with his son, a bloke by the name of McPhee.

271

I was droving bullocks for many years, taking them down to the boat at Derby. We never got anything for any of that work, just a few clothes. A shirt and trousers or something like that. After the cattle were loaded on the boat, we headed back towards the station to meet up with the next mob of bullocks being brought down. We used to take that mob over and bring them into Derby. I was doing a lot of that, so I didn't get back to the station very often.

Then, after we had finished all the droving for the year, we'd go back to the station and start working there. The manager usually put us onto fencing or yard-building. We had to repair the old yards, put in new rails, posts, everything. That was hard work. Some other people would work on the bores, cleaning them out and overhauling the windmill. But we'd have to move all the cattle out into another paddock first, and let them go near one of the other bores. We had to work day and night you know, taking the cattle from one waterhole and shifting them down to a fresh place. That was the hard thing - working day and night, shifting all the cattle round and keeping everything in good working order. The manager and owner never did anything. They kept their hands clean.

None of us got paid in money, we only got clothes and food. We were just like prisoners. Later on we started getting paid 10 bob (10 shillings, about a dollar) a month, but for a long time money never came our way at all, we were working like slaves. They were still working the kids when the money came in. Some only got five bob a month. Some only got two bob. Then when the dollars came in (1966) we started to get a fair bit for stock work. They started paying us 10 dollars a month. But after they brought that big money in, they cut out all the free food and free clothes.

It was hard work mustering by horse, you know. We had to get up early in the morning, get our horses, muster up the cattle, and then tail them all day and watch them all night. We had to cook our own meals too. I took my turn cooking the food for the mustering camp. But the kartiya did nothing. He'd just sit there reading or talking, and he'd sing out, "Horses!" when it was time for the next watch. The blackfella would start work at four o'clock in the morning, working hard while the whitefella was still lying down asleep. We had already done a lot of work before that kartiya even got out of bed.

Derby lean-to camp, early 20th C.

Mustering horses, Leopold Downs.

Jimbo Johnson, Jeffrey Dutchie, Patrick Echo, Desmond Bedford.

Though there was that one kartiya from Queensland, old Victor Jones, who wasn't bad. In fact, he was a good bloke. They called him Milkin. That's Nyikina language for walking stick. He taught me how to spay cows, how to cut the ovaries out. He used to get me, Jock Shandley and one other man who's dead now to do all the spaying. Then we taught a lot of the young fellas how to do it, people such as Tuluk Tighe, Eric Lawford and Chum Lee. All those young fellas.

Victor Jones taught us how to cut out bullocks too. I remember once when he came out to watch us on the job. After sitting down beside his motorcar for a while he said to me, "You know everything. You can do everything." So he went back to the station and let us do the job for him. Then he came back around three o'clock that afternoon to camp with us. He brought everything too, including his own tucker. He asked, "How are the bullocks?" "All right," I told him, "everything is all right." He had a look and said, "OK then. Tomorrow we'll take them down the road." After a while, Emanuel shifted Vic Jones from Christmas Creek and made him the manager at Go Go. He asked me to move to Go Go as well, so I would still be working with him.

I worked with young Emanuel and Victor Jones at Go Go for a while. Then, when they started using trucks for shifting cattle, Victor told me, "You've got to go to Derby. Take all your crew, horses, saddles, everything." So I took six stockmen and went down to Sunnyside.

We waited at Sunnyside till the trucks came with the first load of bullocks. They've got a farm there now, near the Derby aerodrome. That's the place I mean. I was holding a mob of horses there, and when the trucks came they would dump all the bullocks in the yard. They've built that place up a lot now; they've even got a proper farmhouse out there. We only had one little shack out there. Before we built that, we slept there without anything, just on a big bit of canvas. That's all.

Barney Barnes and cattle road train.

At first we didn't have a yard there either, so we'd have to watch the cattle all night. We'd have to tail them on horseback, follow them around and try to quieten them down. The yards were built by the Public Works Department after we'd been there for one or two years. It made the work a lot easier, because we didn't have to be watching the bullocks all night. As soon as the morning came, we'd saddle up the horses, take the cattle out from the yard and feed them in that country around there.

Nowadays they bring in hay, and they can feed the cattle in the yards. But back then we had to take them out of the yards and let them walk around and have a feed. Then, at about four o'clock in the afternoon, we'd bring the cattle back to the yards again. That's the way we used to do it. When the boat came in, we'd take them down to the jetty and load them up. But we used to dip them and inoculate them before they left Myalls' Bore.

Derby jetty cattle yards and steamer

Derby jetty, loading stock from the vessel.

Gibb River chopper muster.

Rugby Yard, Leopold Downs.

I used to meet up with the kartiya down at the jetty. The bloke who delivered the bullocks would give me the waybill, which I'd put in my pocket. When we took the cattle down to the jetty I'd give that waybill to the agent. There used to be a policeman there to check the numbers, the brands and the earmarks of the cattle. He'd have a look around to make sure there were no strangers in the mob, no cattle from another station. Then we'd start running the cattle through the race and onto the ship. We'd work there until all the cattle were loaded.

But the station would often send us too many truckloads of cattle. Five hundred cattle were too many to look after in that place. They'd bring in about 100 bullocks on each of those big trucks. But I didn't like to see those trucks introduced; they did a lot of damage to the bullocks. Not like with droving. Some of those cattle used to die on the truck. When we unloaded them at the yards, there would often be five or ten dead ones. They would have to go down to the rubbish tip and dump them there. Some of the other bullocks were pretty bruised up too. Not like when we were droving them by horse.

I stayed there at the yards working, but some of the other stockmen went back to the station to help with the muster. Different workers came to work under me, but I was there all the time. Truckload after truckload came but I was still there. I was the boss for that place, for all those horses, cattle and everything there at Myalls' Bore. No kartiya used to go there. I did that job for eight years. When we finished with the last lot of cattle for the year, we'd go back to the station and I would start work breaking-in horses. I did a lot of horse-breaking. It was off-and-on sort of work. Each year we'd do a bit of horse-breaking and a bit of other work. They usually took the experienced men off the other work and put them onto horse-breaking.

I finished up with cattle work just after dollars were introduced, I think it was in 1966. I remember young Tim Emanuel came out and said, "You've done a lot of good things for me." Then he gave me $100, just for myself. Anyway, after that, I started working in town with the Shire Council. I started off working on the rubbish truck, and then they put me onto roadwork. I was working alongside all the kartiya, and I even drove the grader sometimes. But I mainly just worked as a truck driver, driving the Shire's old Bedford trucks. I did that Shire job for two years, along with David Mowaljarlai.

So then I started working at the District Hospital in Derby. I worked as an orderly there for three years. Old Nipper Tabagee was working there at the same time as a gardener. That would have been around 1973 I think. After that, I got a job at Numbula Nunga, the old peoples' home. I was employed as a gardener, but I was mainly just watering. Then later they put me into a job as a cleaner. I did that for about a year.

After I finished up at Numbula Nunga, I was a field officer for the Department of Community Welfare, visiting all the people and talking to them about land and everything, to find out what they wanted. We went around all the stations and we talked about anything the people were interested in. We talked about setting up the Land Council. I went around, even up to Kalumburu, Oombulgurri and Wyndham, and right down to Balgo. We had two or three kartiya with us, though I don't remember their names. I worked in that job for three years, and when it finished I stopped work and went on the pension.

I didn't go to any Land Council meetings until that big meeting at Noonkanbah. That Aboriginal bloke, Gularrwuy Yunupingu, who came down from the Northern Territory, and the old men were talking together and they decided to rope me into being on the Land Council Executive. I did a lot of different things with the Land Council before Johnny Watson took over as chairman.

I don't know what they're doing on the stations nowadays. I never learnt anything about the bull-buggy or the helicopter. I finished up before they brought those things in. If I went back to those stations I wouldn't know what the job involved anymore. I might find out there was nothing I could do. And those kartiyas might hunt me out. I don't know, maybe this Government doesn't like the way we did things in the olden days. They want to do it all with a helicopter and bull-buggy now. It's very hard for them to try doing it with horses because it would cost too much money.

Helicopters aren't a good way to muster cattle, but they might be frightened to pay wages for stockmen. They're not offering enough money. They can't buy blackfellas as cheaply as before, so they have to get the helicopter and bull-buggy in. I think money is the reason that they don't want to employ many blackfellas. They might only employ a couple of blackfellas, but that would be all. They mainly employ whitemen. They don't want musterers because nowadays they prefer to fly around in helicopters and drive around in bull-buggies.

It might make the job easier, but it's very cruel, both the helicopter and the bull-buggy. If you round the cattle up with horses, they stay quiet. We used to hold them for a while to let them settle down, and when they had cooled down we would drive them back to the cattle camp with the horses. We might cut out all the bullocks, or something like that. At sundown, maybe about four or five o'clock, we'd put them into the yard. We'd wait till the cool of the afternoon, we wouldn't put them in the yard straight away.

But that's what they're doing with the helicopter, pushing the cattle in from the bush and making them gallop. The helicopter runs them into the yard, and when they're all inside they lock them up. The cattle can't get much room; they get hot and some of them die. I've seen those cattle running in front of the helicopter. The cattle were running in every direction and the helicopter was chasing after them. Some of them would try to break out from the mob, but the helicopter would bring them back. They ran those cattle straight into the yard while they were still hot and their hearts were pumping hard.

That's what's happening now. They just run them into the yard, lock the gate, and leave them there until they're ready to start drafting. Some of the cattle fall down straight away after they're run like that. It kills both bullocks and calves. By the time they get them into the yard maybe half of them are bruised. But that's the new way. Before, it was easy on the cattle, none of them would die like that.

A reach of the Fitzroy River, permanent pool.

Lilly Pool, Kimberley.

We've got a place down in the desert now, a little block down in the country where my father took me walkabout as a kid. It's a good place for cattle and horses, a good place for a garden, and a good place to bring up children. There's a very big waterhole there, so there's plenty of water. The children could walk all round that place. It's a good place for living down there in the desert. I've been back there twice. I went down there after the KLC meeting at Balgo last year. I remember everything down there.

Some Walmajarri people have gone back to that place again, and they're living there now. They want me to go back there. We call that place Ngarantjartu. We're going to get an excision for that place. The Government said, "You can go back to your place if you want to, and sit down there." They said that there would be no humbug; not like before.

Index

284

285

Orthography

The Aboriginal words used in this book are from several different languages. We have followed two principles when spelling these words:
(a) When the established English spelling is known, this has been used.
(b) All other words are spelt using the South Kimberley Language Orthography by Joyce Hudson and William McGregor (shown below).

Pronounce	as in	comments
a	but	not like the *a* in *salt*
aa	path	
i	bit	not like the *i* in *ski*.
ii	beet	
j	jam	
k	koala	often *k* is pronounced like a cross between *g* and *k*
l	lake	
m	money	
n	nothing	
ng	sing, hanger (e.g. Ngalji)	where words contain ngk the *k* is pronounced like *g*
ny	onion (e.g. Kurrkarinya)	ny represents a single sound and should not be pronounced as *n* followed by *y*, as in *many*
p	sip	often *p* is pronounced like a cross between *b* and *p*
r	rotten	not like the r in *car*
rl	no English equivalent (e.g. Kurlku)	sounds like a cross between an *r* and an *l*, though more like an *l* sound
rn	no English equivalent (e.g. Karntipal)	sounds like a cross between *r* and *n*, though more like an *n* sound
rr	no English equivalent (e.g. Marrala	sounds like the rolled *r* used in Scottish English and in languages such as Spanish
rt	no English equivalent (e.g. Kurtany)	sounds like a cross between an *r* and a *t*, though more like a *t* sound
t	sit	often the *t* is pronounced like a cross between *d* and *t*
u	put	not like the *u* in *gut*
uu	boot	
w	wait	not like the *w* in *dawn*
y	yes	not like the *y* in *many*

Aboriginal place names used in Chapter 7
Peter Clancy's story: *I don't have any countrymen there*

Pangnarri	Prior's Yard, Yeeda outstation	Kurrupirrin	Creek on Yeeda
Pangngarrikan	Fraser River (on Yeeda)	Liwan	Four Mile (on Yeeda)
Pangkulmanarn	near Jirrip (on Liveringa)	Manjayi	Calwynyardah station
Bidyadanga	La Grange community	Millijidee	(outstation on Noonkanbah)
Pintinyin	Liveringa station	Ngalji	Mandora station
Jarlmadanga	Mt Anderson station	Nilapaplikan	Nilli Babbaca Well (on Yeeda)
Jinarrkan	Low Broken Wagon (on Mt Anderson)	Palkanjirr	Lower Liveringa (outstation on Mt Anderson)
Jinjirlkan	Nerrima station	Paninypukarra	Paradise, Liveringa outstation
Jirrip	Police camp (on Liveringa)	Purrula	Derby
Kakinpala	Myroodah station	Wungkarlkarra	Udialla
Karrakurtany	Logue Bore (on Yeeda)	Wurrkurra	Warrimbah
Kulakulaku	Luluigui station		(outstation on Noonkanbah)
Kulkarriya	Noonkanbah station	Yawinya	Anna Plains station
Kungkarakarta	Jubilee station	Yuluwaja	Yeeda station

(Facing) Desmond Bedford, Jimmy Echo, Jimbo Johnson, Patrick Echo, Eddy McCoombe, on Mt Barnet

A map of the languages
(after W. McGregor)

JOSEPH BONAPARTE GULF

Miwa

Gamberre   Kwini
Wilawila

Wunambal
Gulunggulu?

Yiiji   Doolboong
Munumburru

Winyjarrumi

Guwij

Yawijibaya

Wyndham   Miriwoong

Worrorra

Wolyamidi

Kununurr a

INDIAN

Ngarnawu
Worla
Walajangarri

OCEAN

Ngarinyin

Jawi

Ord River

Bardi

Umiida
Unggarrangu

Andajin

Kuluwarrang
Kija

Nyul Nyul

Walgi?

Jabirrjabirr

Warrwa
Derby   Unggumi

Nimanburru

Bunuba

Ngumbarl
Jukun

Fitzroy Crossing

Broome

Halls Creek

Yawuru

Fitzroy
Nyikina

Gooniyandi

River   Nyininy

Karajarri

Jaru

Mangala

Juwaliny   Walmajarri

Yulparija

Balgo
Kukatja

Wangkajunga

Gregory Lake   Ngardi

narta

GREAT SANDY DESERT

Kilometres

0   100   200   300

N

Photographic Credits

Page numbers on the left.
Abbreviations — A.I.A.S.: Australian Institute of Aboriginal Studies.
A.R.M., Uniwa: Anthropological Research Museum, University W.A.
W.A.N.: West Australian Newspapers. Jun.: Junjuwa community.

RAPARAPA KULARR MARTUWARRA...

... All right, now we go 'side the river, along that sundown way.